Experiencing Reggio Emilia

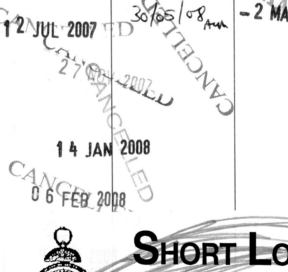

SHORT LOAN

THIS BOOK **MUST** BE ISSUED AT THE COUNTER IF YOU WISH TO USE IT OUTSIDE THE SHORT LOAN AREA

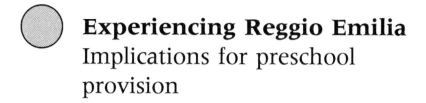

Experiencing Reggio Emilia
Implications for preschool provision

Edited by
Lesley Abbott and Cathy Nutbrown

Open University Press
Buckingham • Philadelphia

Open University Press
McGraw-Hill Education
McGraw-Hill House
Maidenhead
Berkshire
SL6 2QL

email: enquiries@openup.co.uk
world wide web: www.openup.co.uk

and

Two Penn Plaza
New York, NY10121-2289, USA

First Published 2001
Reprinted 2001, 2003 (twice), 2005 (twice), 2007

A catalogue record of this book is available from the British Library

ISBN-10: 0 355 20703 0 (pb) 0 355 20704 9 (hb)
ISBN-13: 978 0 335 20703 9 (pb) 978 0 335 20704 6 (hb)

Library of Congress Cataloging-in-Publication Data
Experiencing Reggio Emilia : implications for pre-school provision / edited by Lesley Abbott and Cathy Nutbrown.
    p. cm.
  Includes bibliographical references and index.
    ISBN 0-335-20704-9 – ISBN 0-335-20703-0 (pbk.)
    1. Education, Preschool–Italy–Reggio Emilia. 2. Early childhood education–Italy–Reggio Emilia. 3. School management and organization–Italy–Reggio Emilia. I. Abbott, Lesley, 1945– II. Nutbrown, Cathy.

LB1140.25.I8 E96 2001
372.21'0945'43–dc21   00-050495

Typeset by Graphicraft Limited, Hong Kong
Printed and bound in Great Britain by Bell & Bain Ltd., Glasgow

To the children of Reggio and the UK, equally 'rich in potential, powerful, competent and most of all connected to adults and other children'.

Loris Malaguzzi

Contents

Notes on contributors

Lesley Abbott is Professor of Early Childhood Education at the Manchester Metropolitan University and head of the Early Years Centre. She was a member of the Committee of Inquiry into the education of 3–4-year-olds, the RSA Early Learning Enquiry and most recently the Government Review of Preschools and Playgroups. She has a particular interest in the role of play in early childhood in multiprofessional training for the early years. She has co-edited a book on early childhood for the Millennium – *Early Education Transformed* with Helen Moylett (1999). Other publications include: with Rosemary Rodger, *Quality Education in the Early Years* (Open University Press, 1994); with Helen Moylett, *Early Interactions: Working with the Under-Threes* (Open University Press, 1997); and with Gillian Pugh, *Training to Work in the Early Years: Developing the Climbing Frame* (Open University Press, 1998). Video and training materials produced by the Early Years Centre include *Firm Foundations* (1996) and *Shaping the Future: Working with the Under-Threes* (2000).

John Bishop is Lecturer in Architecture at the Manchester Metropolitan University and Education Officer at the Centre for the Understanding of the Built Environment (CUBE) in Manchester. He is the founder of the educational charity PLACE which works with children, parents and teachers to promote knowledge and understanding of the built environment.

Robin Duckett was involved in the development of crèche provision in the 1980s. Between 1985–95 he was a nursery teacher in an local education authority nursery school. His particular interests are in the development of the outdoor environment, in family centres and in provision for the under-3s. His innovative work in the Sightlines Initiative has been instrumental in introducing many people to the philosophy and practice of Reggio Emilia. He was responsible for the visit to the UK of the Reggio exhibition in 1997 and organized the study tour from which this book has emerged.

Kath Hirst is an early years researcher at the University of Sheffield. She has considerable experience in both teaching young children and in-service training for teachers, nursery nurses and under-5s workers. She is committed to working with parents both in school and in the community. Her research includes home–school links, working with parents and early literacy with bilingual families.

Caroline Hunter was born in Columbia, educated in Scotland, trained as a teacher in London and taught in Greece and the USA. Since 1980 she has lived in Reggio Emilia where she has taught English as a foreign language and set up a language services agency. She is now a freelance translator and interpreter working for Reggio children. She is parent of a teenager and toddler, both of whom have been educated in Reggio schools.

Cynthia Knight is currently an Early Years Adviser for Birmingham City Council. She has extensive experience in nursery and infant schools as a teacher, deputy head and head teacher. She has written and published papers on early years and school management issues, and has been involved in classroom-based action research.

Jenny Leask was born in Carshalton, Surrey, UK. She has had a number of interesting jobs ranging from civil servant to ships cook. She spent 12 years in Bristol and London as a teacher in special education and moved to Reggio Emilia in 1991. She now teaches English as a foreign language to students from 5 to 60 and works as a translator for Reggio children. Her son is being educated in a Reggio preschool.

Peter Moss is a researcher at the Thomas Coram Research Unit, with particular interest in services for children and their relationship to understandings of childhood. He is also Professor of Early Childhood Provision and was coordinator of the European Community Childcare Network. He has visited Reggio on a number of occasions. His recent publication, *Beyond Quality in Early Childhood Education and Care: Postmodern Perspectives* (1999) with Gunilla Dahlberg and Alan Pence, draws on his experience and understanding of the Reggio philosophy and approach.

Angela Nurse is Director of the Early Childhood Studies programme at Canterbury Christ Church University College. Much of her teaching has been with very young children with special needs, mainly in Inner London and Kent. Before joining the staff of the College, she worked in an advisory capacity with teachers, parents and colleagues in the other statutory services and the private and voluntary sectors. She is a Registered Nursery Inspector and Chair of the governing body of her local school, which includes children with physical impairments.

Cathy Nutbrown is a lecturer in Early Childhood Education at the University of Sheffield, where she directs an MA course in Early Childhood Education. She has considerable experience of teaching young children and working with parents, teachers, nursery nurses and other early childhood educators in a range of group care and education settings. Her research interests include: children's early learning; early assessment; children's rights; work with parents; and early literacy. Her many publications include: *Respectful Educators, Capable Learners: Children's Rights in Early Education* (1996); *Recognising Early Literacy Development: Assessing Children's Achievements* (1997); and *Threads of Thinking: Young Children Learning and the Role of Early Education* (2nd edn, 1999).

Christine Parker is head of a nursery school in Peterborough. She has extensive experience in working with children for whom English is an additional language. She has travelled widely and worked in Pakistan where many of the photographs, which she uses with children, were taken. She is a talented artist and is particularly interested in this aspect of the work of the Reggio schools. She has recently published materials for use with second language learners.

Sylvia Phillips is head of the Special Educational Needs Centre at the Manchester Metropolitan University and of Continuing Professional Development. She leads a European-funded project based in Milan and therefore has wide experience of the provision for children with special needs in Italy. She has published widely in this field and is a member of national committees and development groups.

Wendy Scott is Chief Executive of the British Association for Early Childhood Education. She has had extensive experience as an early years teacher and head teacher, as a tutor on teacher training courses, as an education consultant and as a local authority and Ofsted inspector. She teaches on a wide range of in-service courses for heads, teachers and governors and is an assessor and examiner on nursery nurse and teaching courses. She is co-writer and editor for the Early Years Curriculum Group and edited a paper on early education and care in five European Cities (1996) for the European Commission. She was National Chair of the British Association for Early Childhood Education from 1995–8 and has been Vice Chair of the Early Childhood Education Forum since 1997.

Acknowledgements

Thanks to Trish Gladdis for her skill and patience in the preparation of this book and to our 'Reggio colleagues' for sharing their insight and experiences; and the Institute of Education at the Manchester Metropolitan University and the School of Education at the University of Sheffield for funding and support in order to facilitate this project.

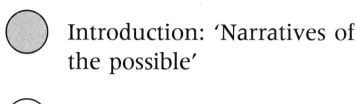

Introduction: 'Narratives of the possible'

Lesley Abbott and Cathy Nutbrown

'The Hundred Languages of Children' exhibition will be, for many, the nearest they get to experiencing the provision of Reggio Emilia. Though the documentation which supports the exhibition is extremely helpful in explaining the *process* of teaching and learning in which children and their educators engage, there is no substitute for observing the settings and the town for oneself, and for face-to-face dialogue with the people who work within the Reggio system. In April 1999, over 100 early childhood educators from the UK visited Reggio Emilia. The study tour included: visits to infant–toddler centres and preschools; lectures from leading educationalists in Reggio; workshops run by Reggio staff; and the opportunity to talk with some staff and parents.

This book is not an account of the first UK study tour experience, but an attempt to consider the pedagogic and philosophical implications of the Reggio approach for early childhood education and care in various parts of the UK. We have compiled this collection in order to contribute to the development of understanding something of the Reggio approach for those working in the UK. As such, it adds to the growing literature written *about* the Reggio Emilia experience (Edwards *et al.* 1993; Gura 1997; Johnson 1999) as well as that written *by* those who work within the Reggio Emilia system.

The contributors to this book include people with a variety of experiences and many different professional roles, including: local authority advisory services, architecture, art education, children's rights, inspection, nursery teaching, play, research, special educational needs and training. The diversity of contributions is reflected in the style of the individual chapters which represent these varied experiences and perspectives. What all the chapters have in common is the fact that they derive from a shared opportunity to observe and explore the theory and practice of early education in Reggio Emilia. Various themes occur and recur throughout the book and we have taken care not to edit out all repetition because the experiences described are key to the perspectives of individual chapters. So, in some chapters themes overlap as authors explore some significant experiences. Reggio educators refuse to be bound by categories that compartmentalize learning and thinking, and similarly the contributors to this book have not confined their reflections to narrow foci, but have drawn on what they saw and felt to construct their own interpretation of Reggio Emilia practice. The structure of this book echoes that ethos of the continuity of experience which is so much part of the Reggio Emilia approach to work with children. We have resisted the usual temptation to 'tidy' the chapters into specific themes; instead the chapters flow, one from another, and we hope unfold some of the questions and excitements, some 'narratives of the possible', which were experienced as a result of studying the work for and with young children in Reggio Emilia.

References

Edwards, C., Gandini, L. and Forman, G. (eds) (1993) *The Hundred Languages of Children – The Reggio Emilia Approach to Early Childhood Education*. Norwood, NJ: Ablex.

Gura, P. (1997) (ed.) Reflections on Early Education and Care. London: British Association for Early Childhood Education.

Johnson, R. (1999) Colonialism and cargo cults in early childhood education: Does Reggio Emilia really exist? *Contemporary Issues in Early Childhood*, 1(1).

1 Experiencing Reggio Emilia

Cathy Nutbrown and Lesley Abbott

What's so special about Reggio Emilia?

Reggio Emilia is a small and historic town in Northern Italy where the Italian tricolour was 'born' on 7 January 1779. During the last quarter of the twentieth century Reggio Emilia became internationally renowned for its provision for young children under 6. It has been a focus of growing interest, attracting visitors from around the globe. The seemingly unique approach to provision, where children from infancy to 6 years of age can learn in community with others, has stimulated much international interest. Presently there are 13 infant–toddler centres catering for children from infancy to 3 years and 21 preschools which offer early education to almost all the town's 3–6-year-olds. The approach to teaching, learning and curriculum is explained in 'The Hundred Languages of Children' exhibition which first came to England in 1997 and toured the UK during 2000.

The experience of Reggio Emilia, in providing challenges to accepted approaches to early childhood education in many countries, is widely acknowledged. Since 1963, when the municipality of Reggio Emilia began setting up its own network of educational services for children from birth to 6 years, the 'Reggio approach' has gained worldwide recognition. Numerous visitors have been impressed by the respect given to the potential of children, the organization and quality of centre and preschool environments, the promotion of collegiality and the ethos of co-participation with families in the educational project.

The Reggio Emilia approach to the education of its young children has grown out of the experience of earlier generations. It has evolved from a resolution to provide something different for future generations, from the growth of the Women's Movement and their desire to make something better for their children. Reggio children of the early twenty-first century are, it seems, inheriting a preschool experience which was conceived when history pointed their grandparents to a different path, and the cornerstones of community and citizenship in the town became the central pillars of the now famously celebrated Reggio Emilia approach to the education of its youngest citizens. These features of community and citizenship in early education prompt Cathy Nutbrown to ask (in Chapter 13) what children in the early twenty-first century might need from their early planned preschool experiences in order to lead full and satisfying lives as world citizens.

Experiencing Reggio Emilia's provision for young children offers wonderful practical ideas: for example, drawing on acetate over light-boxes, using photographic slides in play, reproposing children's language and drawings, and working in groups on projects sustained over time. However, these are simply (simply!) all practical realizations of other more profound theories about children and their learning, of views of children as strong, powerful, competent learners with the right to an environment which is integral to the learning experience. These deeply held beliefs make one ask questions, require deep thought, inner interrogation about what we think, what we believe, and how those thoughts and beliefs are manifest in our work with and for young children. That quality, that capacity to provoke, is perhaps one of the greatest and lasting legacies of any personal encounter with the Reggio Emilia experience.

What do Reggio Emilia preschools look like?

> It is indisputable that schools should have the right to their own environment, their architecture, their own conceptualization and utilization of spaces, forms, and functions.
>
> (Malaguzzi 1996: 40)

Distinctive in all Reggio infant–toddler centres and preschools is the *piazza*: the central meeting place where children from all around the school share their play and conversations together. The tetrahedron with the mirrored interior is often to be found there, with children sitting or standing inside it with their friends, looking at themselves, and many versions of themselves, from all angles. Mirrors proliferate in all the centres in keeping with the central philosophy of 'seeing oneself' and of constructing one's own identity. Another distinctive feature of the Reggio preschools is the *atelier*, the art studio, where children work with the *atelierista* – the experienced and qualified artist who is a member of the staff. The schools are light as a result of the large glass windows from floor to ceiling, and the light, white walls. Colour in the preschool environments is usually the result of children's work hanging from walls and ceilings. Further descriptions of what is to be found in the centres and preschools are scattered throughout this book with several pen pictures of the various environments for learning in the Reggio schools and centres. But perhaps Jenny Leask's impressions (in Chapter 6) of the infant–toddler centre attended by her son is the most vivid portrayal of how the centres look through the eyes of a parent.

Some of the schools are specially built, others have been built for other purposes and later converted for use as a school. Caroline Hunter (in Chapter 5) describes the preschool her daughter attended and the importance of the building in which the children spend their time. Something of the approach to the integral thinking of the architecture of each building with educational practice is discussed by John Bishop in Chapter 9.

Many of the walls of all the centres and preschools are hung with documentation panels tracing the development of various projects undertaken by different groups of children throughout the schools' history. In one school some brightly painted clay masks surrounded a doorway, accompanied by documentation panels which explained the inception and development of the project to make the masks. The work had been done by a group of children who had long since left the school but it remained in the Reggio preschool as a contribution to the learning community; part of the legacy of learning which fills the environment presently being used by the children who now attend the school. The total environment is important in the Reggio system, for as Malaguzzi, founder of the Reggio approach to preschool education, wrote:

> . . . we consider the environment to be an essential constituent element of any theoretical or political research in education. We hold to be equally valuable the rationality of the environment, its capacity for harmonious coexistence, and its highly important forms and functions. Moreover, we place enormous value on the role of the environment as a motivating and animating force in creating spaces for relations, options, and emotional and cognitive situations that produce a sense of well-being and security.
>
> It has been said that the environment should act as a kind of aquarium which reflects the ideas, ethics, attitudes and culture of the people who live in it.
>
> (Malaguzzi 1996: 40)

Who are the Reggio educators?

It is easy to generate the view that the educators of Reggio Emilia are unique people; those we met were articulate and confident men and women who held the shared view of children as competent capable learners, central to their work. Vea Vecchi, an experienced *atelierista* described what underpinned her work with children in an interview in 1998: 'Children have a very basic need to communicate. Their entire day is spent trying to communicate with each other. It isn't always easy. Sometimes they're misunderstood. Misunderstanding can arise not only through a child's choice of words, but also through the listener's expectations of the child' (Gedin 1998: 23). She continued: 'Bringing up children is a social phenomenon. You can't build a good school without the community, without the society. Furthermore, all the different parts of society – the political, the social and the economic – must look at children in the same way, otherwise it's impossible to do a good job in our schools' (p. 25).

During our study tour, we were privileged to meet Vea Vecchi at the Diana School. Her passion for, and deep knowledge of, children and their learning was inspirational. She spent time explaining her work and her processes of documenting children's projects to us, and as she spoke a young woman, newly appointed to work in the school, listened attentively to her every word. This was part of the new *educatore*'s professional development – she was learning about her role alongside an experienced, passionate and committed woman who was firmly grounded in her thinking about children and unshakable in her respect for them. It was as if Vea Vecchi was helping this young woman, a novice to Reggio Emilia preschools, to see children through Reggio eyes, teaching her to 'listen' to the various languages children were using to communicate.

As well as its commitment to developing deep, deep insight of children by 'listening' to them, there are two other striking characteristics of the Reggio approach which make its adults somewhat specially situated to work as they do: *time* and *cooperative working*.

Time

Time to discuss children and their projects is an integral element of the professional role and development of all who work with children in Reggio Emilia centres and preschools. By this means, it seems that the *educatore* and *ateliariste* are 'grown' in the Reggio experience, and in turn further develop the work which centres around the essential view of children as expressed by Malaguzzi, who said:

> Our image of children no longer considers them as isolated and egocentric, does not only see them as engaged in action with objects, does not emphasise only the cognitive aspects, does not belittle feelings or what is not logical and does not consider with ambiguity the role of the reflective domain. Instead our image of the child is

rich in potential, strong, powerful, competent and *most of all connected to adults and children*.

(Malaguzzi 1997: 117, emphasis added)

The educators in Reggio schools and centres spend 6 of their 36 working hours every week without children. This time they spend participating in professional development, planning, preparation and meetings with families – such is the importance given to this spectrum of activity – and in these ways they *stay connected* in their thinking and their approach to being with and working with children and their families. They give children time too – extended periods of time to discuss ideas, develop their cooperative projects, research ways of doing things, try things out, revisit drawings and comments previously made. 'The Hundred Languages of Children' exhibition portrays the processes and outcomes of some of these projects, and it too needs to be given time to fully explore the journey of thinking portrayed in the carefully prepared panels of work and documentation. Christine Parker (in Chapter 10) develops the theme of revisiting – or *reproposing* – children's language and drawings to them over time, describing the effect on her thinking and practice of allowing children time to reflect and transform their words and images should they so wish. Time is an essential ingredient in understanding the work of Reggio Emilia's preschool education – time to read, reflect, think, discuss. In compiling this collection we have benefited, along with the many contributors to this book, from the opportunity to read, think, rethink, reflect, repropose and discuss our images and responses to visiting the work of Reggio Emilia. This experience serves to emphasize, yet again, the importance of time for professional dialogue and development for all who work in early childhood education and care. We could ask what early education in the UK would look like if everyone who worked with young children spent six daytime hours of their designated working week on professional development, planning, preparation and spending time in meeting with families either individually or in groups. Perhaps the Foundation Stage will be fully realized when those who are charged with the responsibility of making it work for children are *required* to spend some of their working day really thinking *together* about the children.

Cooperative working

Cooperative working is the other significant characteristic of Reggio education and care. Teachers always work in pairs, each pair of co-teachers being responsible (in the preschools) for a group of children (Valentine 1999: 3). This cooperative structure of staffing seems to be a realization of the values of the Reggio approach as much as a practical solution to how to work with a group of young children. Co-teaching is a value born out in practice, not simply a way of managing a preschool setting. Working *together*, indeed, *being* together, is deeply rooted in everything that is Reggio: children and parents; children, *educatore* and *ateliariste*; children and children; kitchen staff and children; kitchen staff and *educatore*. During the study tour, staff from the kitchen were observed helping children to water the plants and discussing 'Who is here today?', so that they knew how many places to set for the lunchtime tables. Significantly it was the question 'Who is here today?' not 'How many places do we need?' that was asked first, for the *members* of this learning community (adults and children) were the only reason for needing to know how many places should be set. These overheard conversations were animated, staff and children engaged and at one, because adults were committed to 'listening' to the children. All the adults involved in Reggio preschools and centres seem to work within and live out the same belief in children as 'strong, powerful and competent' members of their community of living and learning *together*.

The community of educators represented in this book have been brought together by their common concern to learn more about children and their learning and to communicate something of their own learning to others. Our experiences are varied, and the paths we have trodden are different. We think differently and, as the chapters illustrate, have seen Reggio Emilia differently. But it is safe to say that we all share the challenge to consider the questions posed to us by the director of Reggio preschools, Carlina Rinaldi (1999). When she addressed us all in Reggio Emilia, she asked:

- What do we hope for children?
- What do we expect from children?
- What is the relationship between school and research?
- What is the relationship between school and education?
- What is the relationship between school, family and society?
- What is the relationship between school and life?
- Is school a preparation for, or part of, life?

These questions lie at the heart of this book, and are embedded in the reflections of the contributors. In writing this book we have interrogated our own thinking, offered some glimpses into the centres and preschools of Reggio Emilia, and some early childhood settings in the UK. Contributors have considered the environments for learning which should be the right of all children, and what might be, given vision and deep, deep understanding and respect for children. In her introduction to the exhibition 'The Hundred Languages of Children' in 1996, the mayor of Reggio Emilia, Antonella Spaggiari, said:

Here on the threshold of the twenty-first century, we have an enormous challenge ahead of us in Europe and worldwide: the challenge
of providing high quality educational services for young children.
The results will be decisive for the future of humankind and for
children's right to happiness. My hope is that this challenge will be
effectively confronted by many countries and governments throughout the world.

(Spaggiari 1996: ix)

This is indeed the international challenge for politicians, policymakers,
researchers, educators, economists and parents – indeed it can be seen as
the responsibility of all adult citizens. The message contained within this
book is that there is something to learn by looking elsewhere. Looking
at Reggio, experiencing Reggio Emilia, has enabled those who have contributed to this book to learn something more and to think again about
the implications our learning might hold for early childhood education
and care throughout the regions of the UK.

References

Gedin, M. (1998) It's just as much about listening . . . an interview with Vea
    Vecchi, *Modern childhood: Discovering the Inquisitive Child Stockholm*, 6: 23–5.
Malaguzzi, L. (1996) The right to environment, in T. Filippini and V. Vecchi (eds)
    The Hundred Languages of Children: The Exhibit. Reggio Emilia: Reggio Children.
Malaguzzi, L. quoted in Penn, H. (1997) *Comparing Nurseries: Staff and Children in
    Italy, Spain and the UK*. London: Paul Chapman Publishing.
Rinaldi, C. (1999) The image of the child. Lecture given at the UK Study Tour,
    Reggio Emilia, April 1999.
Spaggiari, A. (1996) A challenge for the future, in T. Filippini and V. Vecchi (eds)
    The Hundred Languages of Children: The Exhibit. Reggio Emilia: Reggio Children.
Valentine, M. (1999) *The Reggio Emilia Approach to Early Years Education*. Dundee:
    Scottish Consultative Council on the Curriculum.

2

Perceptions of play – a question of priorities?

Lesley Abbott

> On our playground there's some birds who live there, some insects, and lizards too . . . There's some flowers that smell good, lots of trees, big ones and little ones. There's lots of things to play on to have fun, like the climbing thing, and all the places to go around . . . and there's the boat so we can pretend like we're going on a trip.
>
> (Matteo and Naomi – 5 years)

On our last evening in Reggio Emilia a group of us were gathered together, enjoying the balmy April weather and discussing the many challenging experiences and opportunities which the week had offered us. We were in the grounds of the Villetta School prior to going inside to sample, yet again, the warm hospitality of the Italian people and a wonderful meal which will remain in the memory alongside the many other experiences with which our senses had been bombarded during the week.

Close by was a small pond and fountain in which two upturned, brightly coloured umbrellas had been placed in just such a position to allow the water to cascade from the smaller yellow one into the larger red one below. A perspex and wood cube filled with sand contained gaily coloured tubes placed at an angle against the sides to form mini-slides. Rising from the centre was a construction resembling the masts of an old sailing ship to which were attached shiny blue, red and silver windmills which fluttered in the breeze. A tiny bridge spanned the pond and a mini-hammock was suspended from the trees. 'Do you know what this is?' asked the teacher who came to take us inside the school. 'This is the playground for the birds which the children have made for their friends.'

It would be easy to make comparisons between this cool, shady garden and the concrete play areas found in some of our schools. To emphasize the differences between 'us and them' in the value placed on outdoor play, the lack of urgency in planning and developing projects, the support for, and valuing of, children's own ideas and the absence of targets to be ticked off when achieved.

Comparative lists are not difficult to construct and to do so here would make this a fairly unproblematic chapter to write. It would be easy to claim that we never see projects like the 'playground for the birds' in any of our schools and nurseries, that we do not value children's ideas or allow them to engage in activities unrelated to preset goals, but this would be quite wrong. My recent involvement in a local Early Excellence Centre (in which I am currently working) leaves a lasting impression of light and colour, of the richness, competence and creativity of young children and of the commitment, skill and sensitivity of the adults working alongside them. Similarly, filming for our research on the under 3s in a private nursery school in Wales, whose owner had spent some time in Scandinavia and in Reggio Emilia, we were able to capture that 'unreturning moment' when a baby, placed inside the mirrored prism copied from Reggio, caught sight of himself in its different surfaces.

Are there differences then between the definitions, perceptions, provision and priorities in relation to play in the infant–toddler and preschools in Reggio Emilia and those in the UK? If so, what are they? These are important questions, not easily answered by a superficial listing of observable differences.

Matteo and Naomi, quoted at the beginning of the chapter, in describing their playground highlight some fairly significant 'surface' differences, but in order to explore and challenge our own perceptions it is necessary to dig beneath the surface. At the 'surface level' the age of the children is significant. In many parts of the UK most 5-year-olds are in primary school, the majority of them in Reception or Year 1 classes following a 'prescribed curriculum', however favourably we view the Desirable Learning Outcomes (DLOs) and Early Learning Goals (ELGs) (DfEE 1999). Outdoor play for the majority of children of this age is confined to a set 'playtime' in an area, largely concrete, and often shared by many other, much older children. It is unlikely that many of our 5-year-olds will share Matteo and Naomi's view that 'there's lots of things to play on to have fun, like the climbing thing, and all the places to go around . . . and there's the boat so we can pretend like were going on a trip'. Of course there are exceptions, and it may well be that as a result of the welcome references to play in the Early Learning Goals (the introduction of a Foundation Stage from 3–6 years and the development of early years units integrating nursery and reception classes (3–5+)), things are changing.

It is evident so far in this chapter that it is impossible to leave behind years of experience and involvement in many aspects of early childhood education. My involvement in teacher training and in supporting all staff working with young children, my research interests in provision for young children's learning, particularly in relation to play, meant that prior to, during and since my visit to Reggio, these were the areas on which my questions, observations and reading were focused.

The clue to the real difference may be in the ways in which play and education are defined in the two cultures. Traditional views have separated play from work, thus emphasizing relaxation, fun and freedom from concentration as its main purpose with little attention given to the environment in which play takes place. For those working with young children, the value of play has long been recognized but struggles to define, provide and justify it as central to the lives of young children, both in and outside nursery settings and schools, continue for many practitioners.

The environment created and the opportunities provided are central to the ways in which play is allowed to develop and flourish. It is accepted that children will play 'in spite of' and this is true for all children. How much more important is it that the adults who value play as the right of all children should protect and provide opportunities for children to play 'because of'; because of the adults' commitment, vision, understanding and involvement and a recognition that: 'education must come to be recognised as the product of a set of complex interactions, many of which can be realised only when the environment is a fully participating element in education' Malaguzzi (1987: 6).

Tina Bruce is equally convinced of the contribution of the environment as central to children's early learning: 'the child's education is seen as an interaction between the child and the environment the child is in, including in particular, other people and knowledge itself' (1987: 48).

The playground environment experienced by Matteo and Naomi at the Anna Frank School, shared as it is by insects, birds, lizards, flowers and trees is quite different from that experienced by many, but by no means all, of our children in the UK.

Francesca and her friends in their nursery in rural Wales – 'picking daffodils, burying their faces in the yellow, smelling, tasting, running their fingers over petals and trumpets marching and feeling wonderful. Then mixing their colours to paint a profusion of yellow and green – fresh, alive and spontaneous' (Renowden 1998: 112) – surely experienced some of the 'harmonious coexistence' about which Malaguzzi wrote so eloquently and which underpinned the experience of Matteo and Naomi.

Contrast then the experience of Becky – a 5-year-old who had returned to the nursery in Wales on a visit from the primary school to which she had transferred the previous term. When asked by her mother who had accompanied her on the visit, 'Why don't *you* paint a picture too?', she replied: 'I can't'. After much persuasion she painted five straight green stalks and five yellow blobs at the top. The teacher asked, 'What has happened to her confidence, her esteem and creative expression since leaving us?' We might well hazard a guess at what had happened to Becky, and in listing the possible reasons for the changes in her behaviour and response, identify some of the differences in perceptions and priorities in Reggio Emilia and in the UK.

One of the major differences is that in Reggio Emilia Becky would still be in her preschool with a group of children and adults she had grown up with. Although there are between 75 and 90 3–6 year olds in each preschool, and up to 25 children in each class, the homelike closeness and intimacy (often carried over from the time spent together in the infant–toddler centre), provides the children with confidence and a sense of well-being. The fact that children stay with the same teacher throughout the three years enables them, their parents, their teachers and other staff to form strong and stable relationships with each other as members of an extended family and small close-knit community.

In the UK the trauma of transition between home, preschool and school, the different expectations of staff and carers, the system of key workers, quickly replaced by one teacher in a Reception class, the variety of contexts experienced by many children before starting school at 4, can lead to a loss of confidence and identity. Starting formal schooling at an early age, where the 'top-down' pressures to meet externally imposed targets and follow a curriculum designed to prepare children for the next stage in the system, owes more to an industrial model than to that of a cooperative community, so much more appropriate for young children.

Commenting on her visit to a preschool class in Reggio Emilia, Lilian Katz contrasts the approach with that in the USA and highlights the importance of small group-work: 'no evidence was seen of all the children subjected to instruction at the same time, of having to create the same pictures or other art products – a common sight in our schools, especially in connection with holidays like Hallowe'en, Valentine's Day, Mother's Day and so forth' (1995: 32). Sadly it is easy to identify this kind of approach to 'creative activity' in schools where other priorities prevail or where staff may not be appropriately trained to work with young children. Becky's experience may well be of this kind, leading her to doubt her own ability, to rely on externally imposed values and to reject rather than build on the confidence-enhancing experience provided by her nursery.

What *was* evident in the schools in Reggio Emilia was the confidence of the children, not only in their own ability to carry out their plans successfully, to take risks, to take time to pursue their interests, but in the adults with whom they worked and their willingness to support and value their every endeavour.

Tina Bruce (1997: 95) claims that 'even when we travel to foreign places, we take ourselves with us', but she emphasizes that although it is good to travel we must each be ourselves: 'People from different backgrounds need to meet, share talk and dialogue'. Space and time are two important prerequisites in order to 'dialogue' effectively and in Italy the place to do this is the *piazza*. Dahlberg and Asen (1995) report on the *piazzas* in Sweden where politicians, educators, members of the community and parents meet to discuss key issues. In Reggio Emilia the *piazza* is the focal point for young and old to meet, surrounded by cafés, elegant shops, art galleries, churches and the city hall. On Thursdays and Saturdays it houses a colourful, vibrant and bustling market.

Inside the schools of Reggio Emilia the *piazza* or central space has a special place not only as a meeting point for staff, children, parents and other members of the community, but as a focal point for the kinds of play experience which are quite different from those which take place within the classroom.

Almost 30 years ago as a young teacher I was involved in the Schools Council Project – Structuring Play in the Early Years (1974–7) in which over 500 teachers across the country were involved in an action research model of professional development which was well ahead of its time. Not only did it provide opportunities for discussion and debate about play, it challenged thinking and legitimized the inclusion of play within the context of the school. Three key prerequisites for 'successful' play were identified during the discussions which took place in those early days, which have proved to be significant since then, both in my own work and in focusing my thinking about play in Reggio Emilia. They are *space, time* and *materials*. Manning and Sharp (1977: 19) define these three components of play in relation to their views about structuring play as follows:

- *Space*: when teachers allocate certain areas within the classroom or school to specific forms of play, they are imposing a form of structure on that play.
- *Time*: the amount of time children are given to play imposes another form of structure.
- *Materials*: children's play in school is dependent to a certain extent on the materials and equipment available.

A much broader view of play in Reggio is held by Rinaldi who says: 'children must feel that the whole school including the space, materials and projects, values and sustains their interaction and communication' (1990: 137). A similar view is held by Ceppi and Zinni (1998: 16) who consider that 'the spaces, materials, colours, lights, microclimate and furnishings must be direct and integral participants in the great alchemy of growing with a community'.

It would be wrong to say that it never happens this way in the UK. Having recently monitored the transformation of a 1960s open-plan primary school into an Early Excellence Centre where children's need for space, colour, light and texture, both indoors and outdoors, have been guiding principles in the discussion between architects and staff, I am convinced that it does. However, although this is happening more and more in the UK, the difference is that in Reggio Emilia it is the norm rather than the exception.

Vecchi (1998: 129) asks the question: 'what kind of spaces do children need in order to inhabit a school in the best way? In order to discover the answer, research was carried out in the Diana School with children of 3–6 years, focusing on three particular aspects:

- How girls and boys of different ages move in the spaces; what they use them for; what type of relationships the children create in situations in which they organize themselves autonomously in a specific space.
- How girls and boys of various ages perceive and represent the space of the school (inside and out) using different graphic and plastic media.
- How they use sensory channels to make contact with reality and develop their cognitive processes.

Vecchi's research highlights the importance of providing space and time so that children are able to explore relationships and the physical environment. The purpose-built or remodelled schools in Reggio often provide places for children to creep away into private places, hidey-holes, decks and spaces from which adults are banned.

It is not always possible in the UK, as it is in Reggio, to provide such opportunities on a permanent basis in our schools. But it is important that the provision of play, space and experiences which allow for solitary, parallel, group and cooperative activity should be planned rather than the result of a happy accident. Our nursery settings and Early Excellence Centres certainly provide these opportunities and research confirms that children incessantly seek out relationships with their peers.

The connection between space and time

Gandini (1993: 140) comments that:

> when one observes children and adults in the schools of Reggio Emilia one perceives that there is a particular connection between time and space and that the environment truly works. The consideration of the children's own needs and rhythms shapes the arrangement of space and the physical environment, while in turn, the time at disposal allows for the use and enjoyment, at a child's pace, of such carefully thought out space.

Vecchi (1998: 130) observed that 'when the children first arrive in the morning (at the Diana School), they spend most of the time in small groups, trying out relationships, negotiating, exchanging objects from home and planning their games and roles for that day. For those relational exchanges, the older children tend to choose the more remote or secluded areas of the school, occupying all the more 'hidden' spaces.

It is no different for children in our schools; the major difference lies in the time allowed for this kind of activity to take place and in the value placed upon it. In the Reggio schools it is accepted that negotiation, planning play experiences and developing relationships takes time and that these things cannot be hurried. What is important for us to remember is that both physical and mental space is required in order to assimilate and make sense of new experiences. A curriculum which demands that certain goals are achieved within set time limits fails to recognize the importance of providing, valuing and safeguarding space and time.

Jerome Bruner (1998: 137) on visiting a Reggio preschool described it as 'a special kind of place, one in which young human beings are invited to grow in mind, in sensibility, and in belonging to a broader community'. He talks of space and time in terms of 'mine, thine and ours'; and the preschool community as 'a learning community where mind and sensibility are shared. It is a place to learn together about the real world, and about possible worlds of the imagination. It must be a place where the young discover the uses of mind, of imagination, of materials, and learn the power of coding these things together' (p. 137).

For Tina Bruce (1997), 'time to, and for, play' is essential. She warns against too close an emphasis on what we increasingly see in many of our early years classrooms – i.e. play used for the purposes of instruction and socialization. Viewed in this way, guided play, purposeful play, structured play and functional play become a means to an end in achieving specific curriculum goals and targets. Morris (1996: 5) calls this 'a deficiency model demanding the premature practice of what one doesn't know how to do'.

When creativity and symbolic functioning are emphasized, play becomes an activity in which adults are not tied to prescriptive teaching methods, but instead become observers and interpreters of problematic situations. Bruce (1999: 37) talks of the rhythms of play and their ebb and flow, and the fact that children require different help in their play from moment to moment: 'play is not a static equilibrium or a steady state. It keeps changing according to the time of day, the situation and the people (adults or children)'.

The educators in Reggio Emilia clearly share this view, as do the Steiner educators about whom Mary-Jane Drummond (1999: 30) writes, following her observations in a Steiner kindergarten: 'Here as in Reggio Emilia children are encouraged to play because play is seen as important

– really important; not something to be done after work'. She writes about children from 4 to 6 deeply engaged in 'complex, collaborative and imaginative play' and talks about play as 'opening the doors through which children pass as their journeys begin'.

Space and time for play to develop is clearly a prerequisite and, as in Reggio, it is valued and protected in the Steiner schools. Let us hope that the designation of a Foundation Stage for this age group in England will both protect play and allow space and time for it to develop.

What then of materials?

Materials form the third component in the play 'trilogy' identified by Manning and Sharp as far back as 1977. In their study of children's play in England they recognized the role of materials in influencing the kinds of play in which children engage: 'The storage and availability of materials are themselves a form of structuring. Bright, attractive and easily available materials are as essential to stimulate play as they are for other school activities' (1977: 20).

They also recognized the limitations and restrictions under which many children and adults were working over 20 years ago. Although we have learned much more about young children's learning, growth and development and about the nature of play itself in the intervening years, many of those limitations and restrictions still exist. Timetabling of space, clearly defined goals to be achieved within a certain time and designated space, requirements of National Literacy and Numeracy Strategies, Baseline Assessment, Early Learning Goals, testing and inspection procedures all impose severe restrictions on staff who, like the educators in Reggio, believe in 'the importance of an unhurried pace that creates a sense of security, self esteem and the opportunity to work problems through' Gandini (1993: 170).

In a discussion between Leila Gandini and Carlina Rinaldi about the emergent curriculum and social constructivism (Edwards *et al.* 1993: 101) Rinaldi says: 'in our work, we speak of planning, as being understood in the sense of preparation and organisation of space, materials, thoughts, situations and occasions for learning'. Early in the development of their educational programme, the educators in Reggio Emilia appreciated the cultural significance of space. Commenting on their use of space Gandini (1993: 170) says that rather than space being seen as a 'useful and safe place in which to spend active hours' or in the view of Manning and Sharp (1977) as 'structuring educational experiences' it should reflect the culture and history of each centre.

In terms of reflecting their culture and history, my expectation on visiting the centres was that each one would be quite different, and in some respects they were. The buildings ranged from classical buildings such as the La Villetta School, remodelled buildings such as the Diana School, to modern purpose-built structures like the Arcobalena Infant–Toddler Centre. The uniformity for me lay in the materials provided in each school, particularly in the *atelier*, where the same equipment and materials were available for direct investigation and experimentation. These included light-tables, a stimulating variety of artists' materials, clay, paint, tools, inks, brushes, beads and collage materials. Each school is conceptualized as one big laboratory or 'workshop of learning and knowledge'. Staff recognize that pleasure, aesthetics and play are essential in any act of learning and knowledge-building and learning must be pleasurable, appealing and fun.

While it is accepted that a shared philosophy and aims will determine the kinds of resource and environment required in order to facilitate their achievement, I did expect that the culture and history of each individual centre would be more visible. One of the most significant findings for me, with regard to the centres and schools I visited, was the striking uniformity of the central space or *piazza* in each school and the replication of those materials which have clearly become the trademark of the Reggio approach. For example, materials such as mirrors. In particular, the mirrored prism which has attracted so much attention during the visits of the Reggio exhibition to the UK, and into which, when no one was looking, some of us have attempted to squeeze! We observed and noted the different responses of the children we took along with us – the questions asked on seeing themselves and their world from a different angle. On our return many of us have asked handy friends to construct something similar for the nurseries in which we have been working. The circular construction, not unlike the shape of the 'superloo' we see in some of our big cities, in which hang dressing-up clothes of various kinds, hats and capes, bags and shoes to stimulate the imagination and lead to the adoption of new roles and identities, was present in the *piazza* of each school visited.

There was also evidence of what Manning and Sharp (1977) defined as 'structured play' – i.e. the provision of structures, equipment and materials which, although frequently 'subverted' for other purposes, nevertheless suggest ideas about the kinds of play which might take place. For example, in one school there was a large wooden castle of climbing frame proportions with medieval costumes, perspex crowns, chain-mail armour and swords, dresses, pointed hats with flowing veils, goblets and jewels, around which stories could be constructed. The gendered nature of the play in this particular school was also an issue of discussion for us – but quite acceptable in Reggio. In another school, a full-size boat with fishing nets, lobster pots, flippers and snorkels provided opportunities for fantasy play, for holiday experiences to be relived and for parents and staff to share their experiences. The idea of the *piazza* is particularly important in this respect. The central area where meetings take place is a clear instance of the school as a reflection of the society around it.

Bruce (1997: 92) introduces us to the work of the Swiss architect Noschis (1992: 7) who writes about the need for children to play among adults:

> If the child, in moving round in his [*sic*] surroundings, has the chance to brush against craftsmen, shop keepers, clerks, public transportation personnel and enter places such as work places, cafés, shops, bus stops or whatever else constitutes his adult life to be, he also has the opportunity to make them his own and to draw close to these mysteries.

He argues that play should not therefore 'isolate children from the neighbourhood but only be a privileged space for playing what is observed in the neighbourhood' (p. 7).

Plato claimed that children play at what they will do seriously as adults. In this respect the opportunity for children to 'brush against' members of the community whether in the *piazza* within the school or the *piazza* in the world just outside the classroom is an important way of learning about the many different roles played by members of the community. The *piazza* provides an ideal space for these kinds of encounter. Children spill out of their classrooms to engage in play with their peers and to use the variety of materials provided for them. Fewer encounters with adults were observed in this area than in the classrooms, particularly with regard to the adults' role in initiation, participation and intervention in play identified by Manning and Sharp (1977) as being important for children's learning. As Bruce (1997: 92) recognizes, 'the balance of adults and children developing play together is very delicate'. It may be that the kinds of adult–child interaction in play, observed within the classrooms, are viewed by the Reggio educators as 'less risky' in terms of interfering with the children's 'free flow' activity. Adults were observed in classrooms playing chess, acting as shopkeeper in activities clearly designed to develop mathematical skills, helping with the construction of Lego buildings, engaging in miniature world play and puppet play. None were observed engaging in imaginative play with children in the *piazza*. Although their presence was acknowledged by children as they passed through, they were not often invited to stay and play. It is difficult to offer more than tentative suggestions on such a brief visit as to the reasons why this should be so.

Hutt *et al.* (1989) help us to appreciate the complexity of children's play and to recognize that the word 'play' is merely an umbrella term for many different kinds of behaviour requiring a range of adult responses from 'leave it alone' to 'scaffolding and support'. Hutt *et al.*'s distinction between '*epistemic*', knowledge-based play requiring some adult involvement and '*ludic*' fun-based, symbolic, representational play, which often requires adults to stay away, is important with regard to the play observed in the Reggio schools.

It appears that different kinds of play activities take place within different spaces and at different times within the Reggio schools. To return to Vecchi's (1998) research, undertaken in the Diana School, to which reference was made earlier, the first finding confirms the importance of peer relationships and the second the 'confirmation for all ages and for all children of the strong attraction of narrative' (pp. 129–30). Children love to weave stories, projecting themselves into imaginary worlds or simulating real ones. The *piazza* is the ideal place for these kinds of activity to take place. Sadly no equivalent space exists in most of *our* schools. Halls are timetabled for other activities, materials and equipment cannot be left out and classrooms are often quite a distance away. The central space in our open-plan schools, once seen as offering this type of opportunity, is all too often needed for additional teaching space. It is important that space *is* safeguarded for different kinds of play to take place, where children are able to spill out and play; not only as a reward or relaxation from the 'important activities' which schools in the UK seem to be about, but to create a variety of relationships with people and materials.

It is also important that we return to the outdoor playground enjoyed by Matteo and Naomi where this discussion began, and to the playground for the birds created by the children at La Villetta School. An important element of the Reggio philosophy is the recognition of the strong relationship which exists between the inside and the outside of the school building. It would be wrong to deny that educators in the UK are not equally aware of this relationship – we must remember that Malaguzzi owed much to the vision of Susan Isaacs. There are many examples of the creation of outdoor spaces and play opportunities which are challenging and stimulating. The difference is that they are the exception rather than the norm and often educators have to fight long and hard to persuade the powers that be of the value of play, both indoors and outdoors.

Howard Gardner in the foreword to *The Hundred Languages of Children* (1993a: ix) reminds us that: 'Reggio successfully challenges so many false dichotomies: art *vs.* science, individual *vs.* community, child *vs.* adult, enjoyment *vs.* study, nuclear family *vs.* extended family; by achieving a unique harmony that spans these contrasts, it reconfigures our sclerotic categorical systems'. To that list I would add work *vs.* play!

Bruce (1997: 98) challenges us to remember that: 'Children without access to play do not play. Children who have gained access to play then have the courage and daring to play'. We saw many examples of children in whom the courage and daring to play had been fostered. Surely this is what we want for all our children. Howard Gardner (1993b: 107) in his recognition of the 'multiple intelligences' which children possess reminds us that: 'we need to throw out limiting old assumptions and respect the flexibility, creativity, adventurousness, resourcefulness and generativity of the young mind'. First-hand experience of Reggio Emilia helped us to do just that.

References

Bruce, T. (1987) *Early Childhood Education.* London: Hodder & Stoughton.

Bruce, T. (1997) Adults and children developing play together, *European Early Childhood Education Research Journal,* 5(1): 89–99.

Bruce, T. (1999) In praise of inspired and inspiring teachers, in L. Abbott and H. Moylett (eds) *Early Education Transformed.* London: Falmer Press.

Bruner, J. (1998) Some specifications for a space to house a Reggio pre-school, in G. Ceppi and M. Zini (eds) *Children, Spaces and Relations – A Metaproject for an Environment for Young Children.* Reggio Emilia: Reggio Children Modena Domus Academy Research Centre.

Ceppi, C. and Zini, M. (eds) (1998) *Children, Spaces and Relations – A Metaproject for an Environment for Young Children.* Reggio Emilia: Reggio Children Modena Domus Academy Research Centre.

Dahlberg, G. and Asen, G. (1995) Evaluation and regulation: a question of empowerment, in P. Moss and A. Pence (eds) *Valuing Quality in Early Childhood Services.* London: Paul Chapman Publishing.

DfEE (Department for Education and Employment) (1999) *Early Learning Goals.* London: DfEE/QCA.

Drummond, M.J. (1999) Another way of seeing, in L. Abbott and H. Moylett (eds) *Early Education Transformed.* London: Falmer Press.

Edwards, C., Gandini, L. and Forman, G. (eds) (1993) *The Hundred Languages of Children – The Reggio Emilia Approach to Early Childhood Education.* Norwood, NJ: Ablex.

Gandini, L. (1993) Educational and caring spaces, in C. Edwards, L. Gandini and G. Forman (eds) *The Hundred Languages of Children – The Reggio Emilia Approach to Early Childhood Education.* Norwood, NJ: Ablex.

Gardner, H. (1993a) Complementary perspectives on Reggio Emilia, in C. Edwards, L. Gandini and G. Forman (eds) *The Hundred Languages of Children – The Reggio Emilia Approach to Early Childhood Education.* Norwood, NJ: Ablex.

Gardner, H. (1993b) *Frames of Mind: The Theory of Multiple Intelligence.* New York: Basic Books.

Hutt, S.J., Tyler, C., Hutt, C. and Christopherson, H. (1989) *Play, Exploration and Learning.* London: Routledge.

Katz, L. (1995) *Talks with Teachers of Young Children: A Collection.* Norwood, NJ: Ablex.

Malaguzzi, L. (1987) *The Hundred Languages of Children: Narrative of the Possible.* Catalogue of 'The Hundred Languages of Children' exhibition. Reggio Emilia: Comine di Reggio Emila, Assessorato all' Istruzione, Regione di Emilia Romagna.

Malaguzzi, L. (1993) History, ideas, and basic philosophy, in C. Edwards, L. Gandini and G. Forman (eds) *The Hundred Languages of Children – The Reggio Emilia Approach to Early Childhood Education*. Norwood, NJ: Ablex.

Manning, K. and Sharp, A. (1977) *Structuring Play in the Early Years at School*. London: Ward Lock.

Morris, B. (1996) Young children's right to time for play. Paper presented at the IPA Conference, Helsinki, 4–11 August (pp. 1–7).

Noschis, K. (1992) Children's changing access to public places, *Children's Environments*, 9(2): 3–9.

Renowden, H. (1998) Fostering creature and aesthetic development, in L. Abbott and H. Moylett (eds) *Working with the Under-3s: Responding to Children's Needs*. Buckingham: Open University Press.

Rinaldi, C., (1990) The emergent curriculum and social constructivism, in C. Edwards, L. Gandini and G. Forman (eds) (1993) *The Hundred Languages of Children – The Reggio Emilia Approach to Early Childhood Education*. Norwood, NJ: Ablex.

Vecchi, V. (1998) What kind of space for living well in school? in G. Ceppi and M. Zini (eds) *Children, Spaces and Relations – A Metaproject for an Environment for Young Children*. Reggio Emilia: Reggio Children Modena Domus Academy Research Centre.

3

Listening and learning

Wendy Scott

This chapter focuses on the importance of paying attention to all the expressive languages used by young children to represent their thoughts and feelings. It also proposes that adults should listen to each other's differing views. The pursuit of democracy requires us all to respect the differing perspectives to be found between the generations and the diverse groups within our communities.

At the end of the Second World War, the citizens of Reggio Emilia in Northern Italy determined to rebuild their shattered lives. As they emerged from Fascism, they resolved to give their young children a better future. Their philosophy embraced the values and ethics of democracy, and they recognized that these demanded an acceptance of difference and the recognition of others' points of view. Their guiding principle was the need to work in partnership with each other, and to establish a discourse between the generations.

A similar commitment to mutual understanding was evidenced during a UK study tour to Reggio Emilia more than 50 years later. This took place in April 1999, around Liberation Day. During the week, one of the *pedagogistas* spent two long evenings in one of the infant–toddler centres, discussing with staff and parents the issues arising from the situation in Kosovo, which was being bombarded by NATO. The adults' shared concern was how to respond to the questions from the children, who saw TV news, and heard the talk about the situation which was unfolding close to their community. In joining this difficult and sensitive debate, those concerned were living out their belief that the starting point for education must be a dialogue which allows for the exploration of differing views in a climate of trust. The way that parents, practitioners and policymakers in Reggio Emilia listen to each other is actively extended to the children too. The parade along the streets of the town on 25 April was inspiring. The older citizens walked past banners hanging from the public buildings which carried quotations from the young children in the preschool centres, expressing their thoughts about war and peace.

Staff in the centres recognize and celebrate the many ways young children represent their ideas. The importance of paying attention to what children say, and uncovering what they mean, is a key part of the approach to early education in Reggio Emilia. It is facilitated by the meticulous way that educators record the interactions the children have with them. As the pedagogical consultant to the Reggio preschools and toddler centres has commented:

> Documentation as a learning process, but also as a means of communication, presupposes the creation of a culture of exploration, reflection, dialogue and engagement. A culture where many voices – of children, pedagogues, parents, administrators, politicians and others – participate and can make themselves heard, and through that ensure that a multiplicity of perspectives can be scrutinised and analysed. In this way we can open up a way to make sense of pedagogical work for children, parents and pedagogues.
>
> (Rinaldi 1994a: 154)

The community shares a strong belief that children are rich and powerful learners, deserving of respect. This philosophy informs the way that staff, parents and children collaborate in making sense of the world. Documenting their joint enterprises provides children and adults alike with authentic opportunities to put a democratic approach into action. As Rinaldi has stated:

> Children are searching for the real meaning of life. We believe in their possibilities to grow. That is why we do not hurry to give them answers, instead we invite them to think about what the answers might be. The challenge is to listen. When your child asks 'Why is there a moon?' don't reply with a scientific answer. Ask him [*sic*] 'What do you think?' He will understand that you are telling him 'You have your own mind and your own interpretation and your ideas are important to me.' Then you and he can look for the answer, sharing the wonder, curiosity, pain – everything. It is not the answers that are important, it is the process – that you and he search together.
>
> (Boyd Cadwell 1997: 65)

A generation ago, Bruno Bettelheim (1977: 47–8) warned of the dangers of passing on scientifically correct answers to young children's questions:

Realistic explanations are usually incomprehensible to young children because they lack the abstract understanding required to make sense of them. While giving scientifically correct answers makes adults think that they have clarified things for the child, such explanations leave the young child confused, overpowered and intellectually defeated . . . Even as he [*sic*] accepts such an answer, he comes to doubt that he has asked the right question.

Rinaldi (1994a: 153) is clear that openness to children's thinking and learning results in more effective teaching: 'The greater our awareness of pedagogical practices, the greater our possibility to change through constructing a new space . . . it is, above all, a question of getting insight into the possibility of seeing, talking and acting in a different way'.

Loris Malaguzzi, who has done so much to articulate the Reggio approach, declared that a responsive way of working leads to enlightened practice. He emphasized the importance of 'leaving room for learning' by observing children and reflecting, thus enabling teaching to become better than before. He has demonstrated how children's thinking can show the way to the development of a rigorous emergent curriculum. As Santer (1997) observes, the adults in Reggio Emilia are interested not only in what children say and do, but what they mean by their words and actions. Learning in the preschools is about extending and coordinating meanings for all concerned. It involves negotiating what children can find out from each situation as it unfolds. This approach is more demanding than a reliance on prescribed objectives. It can, however, lead to remarkable outcomes, with children achieving at very high levels in all areas of learning, as the exhibition of work from Reggio Emilia testifies.

Vivian Gussin Paley is a leading exponent of a similar child-centred way of working. Her accounts of her approach to teaching at the laboratory school at Chicago University have inspired many practitioners. In *Wally's Stories* (1981), one of her first books, she describes her kindergarten classroom where children are encouraged to learn by expressing their fantasies and stories. The book analyses the evolution of both teacher and students as they grow to understand each other through listening to each other. She shows that, through creating and exploring their own dramatic worlds, 5-year-olds are capable of thought and language far in advance of what they can achieve through traditional classroom instruction. Interrogation, leading to what Katz and Chard (1994) call 'phoney interactive patterns', is not a technique employed in Paley's classroom. Another reflective educator, Cousins (1999) quotes a traveller child who asks his teacher why she keeps asking questions when she already knows the answers – 'Like "What colour is it then?" You can see for yourself it's red, so why do you keep on asking?' To him, remarks like these did not deal with real problems which everyone could puzzle over. In the preschools of Reggio Emilia, the guiding principle for extending children's understanding is to follow the logic of their thoughts, and to create ways in which they can research their own genuine questions.

This child-centred approach relates closely to the traditional British model of nursery education, which has had a strong influence on practice in both the USA and Italy. Although it has not been documented in detail, the emphasis on observing children and taking their ideas and interests seriously has been well established in the UK over many years. The identification of children's own initiatives as the starting point for adult intervention is a significant feature of practice here which has been under threat recently because of a centralized curriculum which underestimates the value of processes of learning. Claxton (2000) affirms the importance of fostering children's confidence and independence, and of helping them to remain flexible in the light of future uncertainties. He relates these attributes to lifelong learning. Interestingly, a learner-centred way of working is now being promoted for education worldwide (UNESCO 2000).

UNESCO (United Nations Educational, Scientific and Cultural Organization) and other international bodies consider access to education to be a fundamental right. The UN (United Nations) Convention on the Rights of the Child states that all children have an entitlement to basic education. Nutbrown (1996) has explored the implications of this, arguing that educators must pay attention to the differing qualities and prior experiences young children bring to their schools and nursery settings. The concept of entitlement to an appropriate curriculum is also integral to the thinking expressed in *Quality in Diversity* (Early Childhood Education Forum 1998), a curriculum framework devised and subscribed to by members of the Early Childhood Education Forum working with children from birth to 8 in a wide variety of settings across the UK.

Although significant developments are currently taking place in early years care and education in the UK, the view of nursery education in Britain is still defined by the government in terms of prescribed outcomes or goals. Funded settings are monitored through an inspection system which does not include advice and support. This attempt at quality assurance is simplistic in a context where many staff are not clear about the goals, and are not equipped to debate their aims with parents and the community. The downward pressure of national expectations, coupled with a lack of understanding of how best to help children to reach the expected goals, tends to result in the adoption of an over-formal approach in many settings. There is then a danger that children may lose confidence in their ability to express themselves. This is avoidable, especially as expert early years educators can demonstrate how to build on pupils' previous experiences, ideas and interests through play. For many years, they have been promoting an inclusive partnership with children and families, and respect for cultural difference. They have tried to include policymakers in an informed discussion about high quality early education, in the knowledge that progress depends on fostering children's motivation to learn.

Their argument is not against raised achievement and goals in themselves, but rather the way that undue emphasis on the end product may devalue the important processes of learning how to learn, and how to turn mistakes to good account. This is particularly important in the UK at a time when there is a growing recognition of the value of early childhood care and education, and a significant expansion of services. There are currently more staff working with under 5s in a variety of roles than there are teachers in the school system. Few, however, are qualified at the levels necessary for them to interpret the goals in ways which will enable children to maintain and develop their motivation and understanding. In these circumstances, it would be useful to focus on the principles and common features of good practice which are included in the guidance for practitioners (QCA 1999). These endorse Malaguzzi's view that teaching will improve when educators leave room for learning and observe carefully in order to understand what children do. As Drummond (1999) points out, educators should listen and record their observations in order to learn to see what children see, and to attend to them as learners.

Bruce (1999) draws attention to the need for spontaneous play and the value of considering salient aspects of a situation from the child's point of view. She observes that one of the dangers of prescribed outcomes is that key processes may be ignored. Peacocke (1999) confirms that children need listeners, and that there are problems where children are in large groups, and where there is pressure towards formal teaching of 5-year-olds. Her call for closer consonance between what is said and what is done highlights the importance of adults taking listening seriously. Indeed, the National Curriculum programmes of study at Level 1 for English are as valid for educators as for pupils:

> to listen, understand and respond appropriately to others, pupils should be taught to:
> (b) ask relevant questions to clarify, extend and follow up ideas
> (e) respond to others appropriately, attending to what they say
> (DfEE 1999)

Unless adults are prepared to pay attention to children's existing experience, and to build on what they already know in the context of their family and cultural backgrounds, there will be continuing mismatches between what is taught and what is learned. The Early Years Curriculum Group asserts the crucial importance of allowing children a wide range of ways of representing their thinking, and emphasizes the view that 'All children need extensive opportunities to think out loud in the language in which they are most competent and comfortable. If we deny them the opportunity, we deny them the right to think for themselves' (1998: 15).

In the rush to extend provision for care and education in the early years in this country, we are in danger of ignoring important considerations. These apply particularly to emotional and social development, which is such an important aspect of children's lives: a working mother reported that when her child cried and clung to her as she left for work, she convinced herself that he would be fine once she was gone. It was too inconvenient or threatening for her to 'hear' his distress (Neustatter 2000). She came to recognize that her child was paying the price of her ambition, and has not regretted her decision to alter her pattern of work in those crucial early years.

Many parents will relate to her dilemma, and know that the current expansion is as much about freeing women to join the workforce as it is about young children's entitlements to high quality care and education. The common difficulties related to early entry to school and the discontinuities in provision for their care and education experienced by too many children in the UK lead to insecurity, and contrast uncomfortably with the child-centred approach adopted in Reggio Emilia. There were consistent warnings about the dangers of imposing too formal an approach too early in recent television programmes and in the published findings of the Parliamentary Select Committee for Education during the 1990s. The recommendations of the Rumbold Report (DES 1990) were endorsed over this period by the National Commission on Education (1993) and *Start Right*, the report of the Royal Society of Arts Early Learning Inquiry (Ball 1994). The undesirable consequences of too much adult-directed practice in the early years have not yet been recognized in influential quarters, in spite of compelling evidence of negative effects, especially on boys.

However, although concerns remain, particularly about the inspection régime, there are hopeful developments. The national evaluation of the Early Excellence Centres is based on self-assessment. Local evaluators take on the role of critical friends, similar to that of the Italian *pedagogistas*. They are trusted as experts, and share their expertise, paying attention to the areas of development identified by the Centres themselves. There are other indicators that a more responsive approach is being adopted: Sure Start is growing from community-based projects, and is intended to give local people a voice in developing what they need for the youngest children and their families. Early Years Development and Childcare Partnerships are opening up the possibility of local definitions of quality, and of devising training to match the perceived needs of local provision. A start has been made on a framework for qualifications which will rationalize the accreditation of existing childcare courses, and early years has been recognized as a distinctive specialism comparable to subject specialisms in teacher training (Abbott and Pugh 1998).

The Early Learning Goals set for children at the end of a proposed Foundation Stage (QCA 1999) are embedded within principles and aims which emphasize dispositions to learn and other related longer-term outcomes. The importance of play is acknowledged, and the value of children's spontaneous ideas and initiatives is endorsed. All of this is consistent with the findings of brain research (Shore 1997), and will help practitioners to counter any pressures towards the imposition of unsuitable formal practice too soon. Like the parents and educators in Reggio Emilia, they will be able to set the foundations of lifelong learning. Parker-Rees asserts that: 'policy can grow down if it responds to the interpretations of the practitioners . . . and we can all grow down if we can still the clatter of our minds long enough to let us listen to the undermind roots which inform our thinking' (1999: 70).

In arguing for enlightened policies, Dahlberg *et al.* (1999: 148–9) propose that

> the view of children as co-constructors . . . of knowledge is fundamentally important. It is quite at odds with the 'banking' model of learning and the child as re-producer of predetermined knowledge. It understands that what children learn, all their knowledge, emerges in the process of self and social construction since children do not passively endure their experiences but become active agents in their socialisation, co-constructed with their peers. It is a view of children as meaning makers. But always in relationship with others, seeking an answer, rather than the answer.

David (1999) draws attention to the relevance of society's construction of childhood, and comments that children live up – or down – to societal and family expectations and will try to please the adults around them in order to be loved and accepted. She affirms the imperative of valuing children as tomorrow's citizens with a voice of their own. As she points out, the Children Act 1989 required that we act in the best interests of the child, and heed the child's views. Endorsing these points, Dahlberg observes that: 'early childhood institutions carry great symbolic importance. They are statements about how we, as adults, understand childhood and its relationship to the state, the economy, civil society and the private domain' (Dahlberg *et al.* 1999: 86). In this context, it is worth returning to the community of learners in Reggio Emilia, and the cornerstone of their approach, based on principle, research and experience. They believe that young children are rich, strong and powerful and that they have:

the desire to grow, curiosity, the ability to be amazed and the desire to relate to other people and to communicate . . . children are eager to express themselves within the context of a plurality of languages . . . children are open to exchanges and reciprocity as deeds and acts of love which they not only want to receive but also want to offer.

(Rinaldi 1994b: 112)

We can all gain from responding to the subtle, generous and thought-provoking communications offered by the young children in our care. It is our responsibility to create places where they can express themselves confidently, sure of a sympathetic hearing. We owe it to the next generation to listen to their ideas and to pay attention to their views, and thus to foster significant personal development as well as measurable educational outcomes. Carlina Rinaldi inspired the group of educators from the UK who were in Reggio Emilia in April 1999 when she said:

if we believe that children possess their own theories, interpretations and questions and that they are protagonists in the knowledge-building processes, then the most important verb in educational practice is no longer to talk, to explain, or to transmit, but to listen. Listening means being open to others and what they have to say, listening to the hundred and more languages, with all our senses. Listening means being open to differences and recognising the value of different points of view and the interpretation of others.

(Rinaldi 1999)

An important lesson for all of us – the pedagogy of listening opens up a way of life.

References

Abbott, L. and Pugh, G. (1998) *Training to Work in the Early Years – Developing the Climbing Frame*. Buckingham: Open University Press.

Ball, C. (1994) *Start Right: The Importance of Early Learning*. London: Royal Society for the Encouragement of the Arts, Manufacturers and Commerce (RSA).

Bettelheim, B. (1977) *The Uses of Enchantment*. New York: Vintage.

Boyd Cadwell, L. (1997) *Bringing Reggio Emilia Home: An Innovative Approach to Early Childhood Education*. New York: Teachers' College Press.

Bruce, T. (1999) In praise of inspired and inspiring teachers, in L. Abbott and H. Moylett (eds) (1999) *Early Education Transformed*. London: Falmer Press.

Claxton, G. (2000) A sure start for an uncertain future, *Early Education*, 30: 41–4.

Cousins, J. (1999) *Listening to Four Year Olds: How They Can Help Us Plan Their Education and Care*. London: The National Early Years Network.

Dahlberg, G., Moss, P., and Pence, A. (eds) (1999) *Beyond Quality in Early Childhood Education and Care: Postmodern Perspectives*. London: Falmer Press.

David, T. (1999) Valuing young children, in L. Abbott and H. Moylett (eds) *Early Education Transformed*. London: Falmer Press.

DES (Department for Education and Science) (1990) *Report of the Committee of Inquiry into the Quality of the Educational Experience Offered to 3- and 4-Year Olds* (chaired by Mrs Angela Rumbold CBE MP). London: HMSO.

DfEE (Department for Education and Employment) (1999) *Programmes of Study for English*. London: HMSO.

Drummond, M.J. (1999) Another way of seeing: perceptions of play in a Steiner kindergarten, in L. Abbott and H. Moylett (eds) (1999) *Early Education Transformed*. London: Falmer Press.

Early Childhood Education Forum (1998) *Quality in Diversity*. London: The National Children's Bureau.

Early Years Curriculum Group (1998) *Interpreting the National Curriculum at Key Stage 1: A Developmental Approach*. Buckingham: Open University Press.

Gussin Paley V. (1981) *Wally's Stories*. New York: Harvard University Press.

Katz, L. and Chard, S. (1994) *Engaging Children's Minds: The Project Approach*. Norwood, NJ: Ablex.

National Commission on Education (1993) *Learning to Succeed*. London: Heinemann.

Neustatter, A. (2000) I'll never regret trading my job for my children, *Observer*, 30 January.

Nutbrown, C. (ed.) (1996) *Capable Children, Respectful Educators: Children's Rights and Early Education* London: Paul Chapman Publishing.

Parker-Rees, R. (1999) Protecting playfulness, in L. Abbott and H. Moylett (eds) *Early Education Transformed*. London: Falmer Press.

Peacocke, R. (1999) Inspecting the future, in L. Abbott and H. Moylett (eds) *Early Education Transformed*. London: Falmer Press.

QCA (Qualifications and Curriculum Authority) (1999) *Early Learning Goals*. London: DfEE.

Rinaldi, C. (1994a) Observation and Documentation. Paper given at the research conference, Reggio Emilia, 28 April.

Rinaldi, C. (1994b) in C. Edwards, L. Gandini and G. Foreman (eds) *The Hundred Languages of Children – The Reggio Emilia Approach to Early Childhood Education*. Norwood, NJ: Ablex.

Rinaldi, C. (1999) The pedagogy of listening. Paper given in Reggio Emilia, 28 April.

Santer, J. (1997) Respecting children and their disposition to learn, in P. Gura (ed.) *Reflections on Early Education and Care*. London: BAECE.

Shore, R. (1997) *Re-thinking the Brain: New Insights Into Early Development*. New York: Families and Work Institute.

UNESCO (United Nations Educational, Scientific and Cultural Organization) (2000) Papers from Education for All, the Regional Conference for Europe and North America, Warsaw, 6–8 February.

Quality and the role of
the *pedagogista*

 Cynthia Knight

What she does is raise questions with us. When she comes we just
talk, constant talk all the time.

As an early years adviser in the UK one of my major interests in visiting
the Reggio schools was in the role of the *pedagogista*. The aims of this
chapter are therefore to:

- explore the role of the *pedagogista* in supporting the development of
  quality in the schools in Reggio Emilia;
- compare the role of the *pedagogista* with other models of outsider
  intervention in school improvement and in-service training;
- examine the implications of the *pedagogista* role for UK practice with
  early years practitioners.

There is no question that the children in the preschools of Reggio
Emilia achieve remarkably high standards in a variety of areas: in their
observations and understandings of the world; in their creativity; in
their ability to work collaboratively; in their emergent understandings of
citizenship. How then is this achieved? In this chapter I investigate some
of the elements of the Reggio approach in the light of recent research
about successful organizations, including schools. I begin by exploring
some recent research into the characteristics of successful organizations,
describing the important role of the *pedagogista* and finally discussing the
relevance of this role to practitioners in the UK. Recent research into
organizations has emphasized the importance of a variety of factors,
which contribute towards achieving high quality, and it is significant
that many of the elements are in place in Reggio Emilia.

Fullan (1999: 13) describes some of the characteristics of successful
organizations as 'committed to creating collaborative, problem solving
communities, with a commitment to knowledge building'. He further

states: 'the living company was characterised by much greater sensitivity to the chemistry of people within the organisation, and to the evolution of, and relationships with its external environment'. However, although the emphasis was on collaboration and sharing ideas, diversity and conflict are seen as an important part of the ongoing dialogue: 'true dialogue in which people engage with each other not to be in control but to provoke and be provoked to learn and contribute to the learning of others, to change their own minds as well as the minds of others' (Stacey 1996: 280).

In his description of the internal workings of successful schools, Fullan (1999: 14) highlights the importance of a direct focus on pupil learning by all staff: 'Teachers as a group examine together how well students are doing. They relate this to how they are teaching, and make continuous refinements individually and with each other'.

The relationship between the school and the outside world is highly significant for those in the Reggio schools. The symbiotic nature of this relationship is emphasized by Fullan (1999: 16):

> The secret of learning communities is that they consist of intricate embedded interaction inside and outside the organisation which converts tacit knowledge to explicit knowledge on an ongoing basis . . . However these interactions must yield quality ideas which must be shared and used throughout organisations. In this way by knowing themselves, they are able to explain themselves with greater confidence when dealing with outside in their quest for continuous improvement.

The high value placed on relationships with parents and community is apparent in Reggio and is seen by Fullan (p. 46) as a feature of high achieving schools:

> Schools maintain a sustained focus on strengthening the involvement of parents with the school and their children's schooling. They actively seek to strengthen the ties with the local community, and especially those resources that bear on the caring of children . . . Greater trust and mutual engagement begins to characterise these encounters.

Interaction at all levels and between many 'stakeholders' including parents, children, staff and the wider community is at the heart of the Reggio philosophy: 'The interactive systems – the deep meaning of collaboration to obtain substantial results – are precisely systems that gain their tremendous energy through the fusion of intellectual, political, spiritual purposes. At their best they do this at the individual, organisational and system levels in concert' (Fullan 1999: 82).

Any visitor to Reggio Emilia would be able to identify all the elements of success identified by Fullan and other researchers into school improvement. Namely:

- the professional community dedicated to raising questions and problem-solving about children's thinking and learning;
- the emphasis on diverse and sometimes conflicting views as part of the search for new understandings for both children and staff;
- the integration of parents and the community into the learning organization;
- the ability of all participants to talk confidently about processes;
- the symbiotic relationship between schools, parents and city;
- the use of knowledge from outside through access to research and contact with other countries;
- the fusion of moral, political and intellectual elements.

The role of the *pedagogista*

The missing factor here is the complex role of the *pedagogisti* as an essential element of the success of the schools in Reggio. The *pedagogisti* provide a fundamental link between all the participating elements mentioned above in a unique way and one which differs in many ways from that of the early years adviser or advisory teacher in the UK.

In Reggio Emilia, the *pedagogisti* play an essential role in enabling all the processes to develop and continue. They are both insiders and outsiders. Insiders in that they facilitate focus and reflection on the evidence about children's learning, which is gained from detailed recording or documentation. Outsiders in that they encourage the collaboration between settings and parents, the community, the town and of course the wider Italian and international community, through visits, discussions and seminars.

In order to develop and maintain the consistently high quality of all the nurseries in the town, each *pedagogista* is responsible for only a small number of settings. They visit each early years centre once a week, working to create a relationship, not just with teachers, but also with children and families. They engage in problem solving in the context of real situations, enabling teachers and parents to offer solutions and raise further questions that are real and pertinent to the particular children and families in the centre. *Pedagogosti* bring high levels of expertise, encouraging children, teachers and parents to explore different perspectives, rethink situations and revisit experiences – namely, to be reflective.

To support this culture of collaborative evaluation and research, teachers have annually 190 hours outside the classroom, 107 of which will be dedicated to in-service training, and 43 to work with parents. The rest is spent in discussion of projects and documentation of children's work.

Each *pedagogista* plays an important role in helping teachers to improve their skills of observing and listening to children, documenting projects and conducting their own research. Staff in the nurseries are also supported in identifying their own in-service development needs, and the *pedagogista* is involved in helping to ensure that these needs are met.

Teachers are also encouraged and supported by the *pedagogista* to enhance their skills in relation to their work with parents, to enable them to talk and listen. For example, the *pedagogista* may observe a child, then discuss these observations with the teacher and the parent, in order that they can successfully support the child through the next stage of their learning. In the same way as the image of the child is one of competence (the subject of rights, rather than needs) so the aim for teachers is for autonomy, while at the same time maintaining a focus on collaboration and problem solving.

In addition, the importance of relationships with the town and other agencies cannot be overstated. In order to discuss policy, raise issues and share theories and current research, *pedagogisti* meet with the director and other colleagues weekly. Links with the wider community through receiving visitors, and engaging in dialogues and research with international contacts, are also an essential feature of the culture of perpetual review, problematizing and the creation rather than simply the transmission of knowledge.

A *pedagogista* is therefore able to operate in a holistic way which provides consistency of quality across the settings in a climate of self-review, evaluation and research, whether it is at individual child, family, school or town level.

Quality in the UK

Many different systems of quality development and control exist concurrently in the UK, even for children of the same age. Early years settings may be subject to different inspection frameworks. Nationally appointed and local advisers and inspectors fulfil a monitoring role, some offering advice and support. The frequency and depth of this support will vary according to the perceived quality and needs of the setting, and the human resources available in a particular region or area. Mentor teachers may be responsible for offering curriculum advice to a number of early years settings functioning without a teacher. A variety of self-review and improvement procedures are be available to individual settings. The Office for Standards in Education (Ofsted), Her Majesty's Inspectorate of Schools (HMI) and local authority inspectors regularly report on quality issues in the various sectors. Hence, achieving consistency across all these different models is a complex challenge, particularly in the light of the huge expansion in early years provision which is currently taking place in the UK.

Many early years settings and schools have already achieved high standards in terms of the quality of their provision. How have they done this? What are the factors which have contributed to this success? Do they relate to those highlighted by Fullan (1999), and could the notion of the *pedagogista* have any place within the development of coherent quality in UK early years education?

In the local authority in which I work, heads and managers representing a variety of settings, which had received excellent inspection reports, were invited to discuss the issue of quality development. Many common themes emerged, and most related directly to the elements already referred to by Fullan (1999) and which are embedded in the pedagogy of Reggio Emilia.

Well-being for both staff and children was seen to be essential, and one head teacher commented:

> I suppose there are many ways of monitoring quality. You know, the feel of it in terms of interactions and relationships, whether the children and staff are working well together. We're doing some deeper work on well-being . . . measuring it. Everyone is involved in it. The good thing about that, is that it raises the quality immediately. Because, of course, nobody is going to notice a child who is low down on the 'well-being scale' [Laevers *et al.* 1994] and not do something immediately about it.

All heads were very clear about their major role in constantly facilitating discussions about the pedagogic philosophy with all their staff, and this is seen as an extremely important function for the *pedagogisti* in Reggio. This was not seen as a one-off process but as an ongoing responsibility. The critical importance of giving parents, new staff and visitors an insight into the process was repeatedly emphasized.

Children's learning was the major focus for all the settings and as staff commented: 'Everyone looks at children's involvement and interaction all the time. Staff make time for observations. We are constantly talking about the children. We are always developing and reflecting on aspects which need changing in the nursery in response to different groups of children'.

All the heads emphasized the centrality of the idea of 'the learning community' and in exploring the creation of a 'professional ethos' with one head, she commented:

> We have set very firm ground rules about being professional. It's what we would expect of the children. For example, not gossiping about people, not being unkind, not talking about them behind

their backs. If there are issues, there are ways of dealing with them. If someone shares something personal with you, you would not share that with someone else.

The importance of constant discussion about ideas, and the raising of questions, was a feature referred to by all heads consulted. For example:

> I do spend a lot of time talking with staff, and now they are feeding it back to me. I mean it's much more a two-way process. Because they're becoming more confident and reflective – of course they are raising the questions now.
>
> I try to recruit staff who are open and receptive. They have the skills to work with the children, but also the intellectual openness to try out new ideas – most of us are doing further study. That's important because it brings in other trains of thought and theories.

All settings were committed to lifelong learning not only for all staff but also for parents: 'It's just like children's entitlement. I do believe in lifelong learning. Everyone is entitled to have somebody they can reflect with, talk things over, or access something for them'.

The view of the practitioner as action researcher was shared by all the settings. They had all taken part in several research projects and initiatives, the findings of which they had acted upon, and integrated into their own systems and knowledge base.

Although all settings were relatively confident about their ability to monitor quality, most were strongly committed to the idea of a common self-evaluation framework. Particular mention was made of the Effective Early Learning Project (Pascal *et al.* 1994). This is a national project, which gives settings the opportunity to evaluate themselves using ten dimensions of quality. The close focus on directly observing learning and teaching, with moderated criteria, was seen as a very positive feature of the process. Other aspects of the project valued by heads were the external adviser support, and the opportunities to discuss issues with groups of early years practitioners on a regular basis. All the settings have integrated many aspects of the project into their own ongoing self-evaluation processes. One of the heads remarked: 'It has helped us develop a way of thinking. It's helping us to sort out what we are really about. We all had different ideas and interpretations. It has empowered staff to talk about what they believe about children's learning'.

All the heads were emphatic that regular external support of different kinds had been an important factor in the development of quality. Although most recognized that external monitoring was necessary, it was in the discussions about the *pedagogista* and the mentor role that most enthusiasm was shown. One of the schools had been supported by a researcher over several years: 'What she does is to raise questions with us. She never criticizes us. When she comes we just talk, constant talk all the time. Then she will go away and send research papers to us'. The development of the mentor teacher role, to support settings without a teacher in the early years, has been a particularly interesting phenomenon over the past two or three years. All the heads of the settings involved in the discussions about quality had been involved in such a scheme, either by receiving support from a mentor, or as mentor teachers themselves.

In the particular scheme familiar to the heads, mentors aimed to establish similar kinds of relationship as those of the *pedagogista*, working closely with staff to reflect on the teaching and learning. When asked whether a self-evaluation programme on its own was sufficient, one head of a successful setting said:

> No I don't think it's enough. It's not enough on its own. We have the teacher mentor . . . that's been a really good scheme and it's worked really well here because it's somebody else coming into your establishment, working on our agenda as well. But also they've got loads of experience . . . a wealth of knowledge and experience of managing departments and managing other early years settings in other nurseries and schools. And they're involved on a very practical level within the nursery. They get to know the staff really well. They get to know the children. They advise us on our topics and our planning. We've got a common language with them. The staff relate very well to her [the mentor] . . . they are really receptive and have a lot of respect.

Another head, who is also a mentor, talked about the relationship she was establishing with her group of settings:

> So really a lot of it is about establishing relationships. And not being judgemental. I mean I feel really strongly about this issue of not being critical. There's that quote about children, which says that if you criticize a child once, it takes at least ten positives to make it up. I try to raise questions with them. Often they will raise the questions . . . but I keep checking and say how do you feel about that. I've moved more and more towards really trying to get them to identify the questions.

The mentor teacher role is in the early stages of development. At present, mentors rarely work with parents in the way that the *pedagogisti* do in Reggio. However, when this idea was put to heads with mentors, and also mentor teachers themselves, they were unanimously enthusiastic. Unfortunately, financial constraints have so far not allowed mentors to devote as much time to individual settings as the *pedagogisti* in Reggio Emilia. They must divide their time between many settings, some with no teachers and others where teachers have expressed an interest in having the kind of stimulation which a *pedagogista* provides.

One of the heads suggested that mentors might work with a small number of settings in a particular community, whether they were maintained or private. This would ensure the sharing of expertise, the moderation of quality and high impact on parental participation and partnership. This would fit well with the current ideas and new government initiatives such as Sure Start and Early Excellence Centres.

Conclusion

At a time when the focus on the early years has never been so strong, it is important to seize the moment and research the experiences of successful organizations both in the UK and abroad. Although it is evident that the way in which childhood services develop in different countries is dependent on political and cultural contexts, there are many successful processes at work for the children, the practitioners and the parents which can be shared, documented, experimented with, challenged and discussed. In the interest of high quality it is essential to continue to raise the questions.

The current emphasis for schools in the UK is on achieving outcomes. All the heads interviewed had achieved what was required of them by nurturing a complex web of relationships both inside and outside their organizations. They were also still determined to continue to improve quality for children and adults, and were committed to the idea of the developing role of the *pedagogista* or mentor.

Acknowledgements

The opinions expressed in this chapter are those of the author who would like to thank the heads, who gave up some of their precious free time to talk to her.

References

Fullan, M. (1999) *Change Forces: The Sequel*. London: Falmer Press.

Laevers, F., Vandenbussche, E., Kog, M. and Depondt, L. (1994) *A Process Oriented Child Monitoring System for Young Children*. Leuven: Centre for Experiential Education and Leuven University Press.

Pascal, C., Bertram, A. and Ramsden, F. (1994) *The Effective Early Learning Research Project: The Quality, Evaluation and Development Process*. Worcester: Worcester College of Higher Education.

Stacey, R. (1996) *Complexity and Creativity in Organizations*. San Francisco: Berrett-Koehler.

5 Sunniva's extra pocket – a parent's reflections

Caroline Hunter

My name is Caroline Hunter. I have been living in Reggio Emilia for nearly 20 years after having trailed the world as a child in a large diplomatic family and also on my own account. I trained as a teacher in London after boarding school in Scotland and taught in London, Bristol and Greece before coming to Italy. Despite the climate I am still here in Reggio Emilia and pleased to herald the considerable advantages living in the town offers – it is a good place to bring up children and I feel very happy about having been clever enough to have my babies here.

My eldest daughter Sunniva, now 16, started at her infant–toddler centre when she was 9 months old. I was then a single, self-employed foreign mother with no choice but to find provision for my baby while I worked. I rather took for granted the fact that local authority provision for such a small child was so readily available and cheap, but came swiftly to realize that the infant–toddler centre (*asilo–nido*) was not just going to be a safe, convenient and clean place to leave my baby, but a rich, rewarding and supportive experience for us both.

To begin with, I liked the name, *Asilo–Nido 'Arcobaleno'*, literally: Rainbow Nest Shelter – a colourful place in which safely to grow. I found the school environment immediately both stimulating and welcoming, inviting one to wander through the whole interconnecting space, exploring and discovering. The staff, particularly the two teachers in charge of Sunniva's group, were all extremely open and friendly in all their dealings – we used the familiar *tu* form when speaking right from the start. At the beginning I spent the first few days with Sunniva at Arcobaleno. We stayed for just a short time the first day and gradually lengthened the time. Then I began by going away for half an hour and slowly increased the amount of time I stayed away until she was staying the entire day there from 8 a.m. to 4 p.m. The staff were entirely flexible on this introduction period, the aim being the establishment of secure relationships between the child, the staff, the parents and the environment.

At no point did I feel even slightly stigmatized due my status – exactly the contrary, the staff were all genuinely interested in our 'difference', were quick to pick up on how this could contribute to enriching the school's life and soon had me singing in English at school parties. All the parents were encouraged to bring whatever skills or interests they may have to school for the benefit of the environment and the enhancement of our common experience.

If I had been impressed by the amount of information I had to provide about Sunniva at the first meetings with the school staff this was quickly outweighed by the sheer quantity I was offered regarding almost her every move throughout the day. Easily consulted charts spelled out what and when and how much she had eaten, the change frequency and contents of her nappies as well as the activities she had been involved in and any other special observations regarding her day. On a practical level this was extremely helpful for the organization of the rest of our day together and also made me feel involved in her day and able to talk with her about it. Flexible entry and leaving times meant that the teachers were happy and available to chat and exchange information if anything needed clarification. The adult-sized sofa in the entrance area invited one to linger and share a few moments of the day in school together as well as meet and talk to other parents.

Parents were encouraged to become closely involved in school life; class parent and teacher meetings were held regularly and parent participation and observations greatly encouraged lively discussion. I particularly liked the lack of hierarchy in the staffing system; all the staff including non-teaching staff were valued for the important and individual contribution they made, and parents and children were thus completely natural in talking to the cook and the cleaning staff about the school as much as to anyone else.

There was a very natural feel to the way that the children's activities developed and changed. The apparent lack of formal structure to the activities belied the careful selection of materials and situations that were offered to the children to respond to. My impression was that my child was being very carefully 'listened' to and that each avenue explored was a new voyage of individual as well as collective discovery. Beautifully displayed large panels illustrated the children's activities and development clearly; at the end of each year we were given a thick volume of photographs, commentaries and creative work which Sunniva looks at to this day. I am particularly grateful to the infant–toddler centre for these lasting records; as I was working more than full-time

I never had as many opportunities as I would have liked to document Sunniva's first years myself.

After three years at the infant–toddler centre, I had to make a fresh application for a place but happily Sunniva went on to my first choice preschool. Once again I had a meeting with her teachers before the school year started to talk about Sunniva, her habits and preferences. A chart of information was passed on to the preschool from the infant–toddler centre after being shown to me for discussion and approval. The preschool was a perfectly smooth follow-on from the infant–toddler centre experience, and many of the children Sunniva had been with at the infant–toddler centre came to the same school. This time I was prepared for and expecting the open, friendly and stimulating exchanges with the teachers and non-teaching staff, and we soon felt greatly at home in the new environment. At this stage it became even more apparent how the 'projects' the children worked on were the fruit of their own curiosity and will to explore. One boy bringing a spaceship to school led to the collective construction of a huge moon landing vehicle along with the exploration of other connected activities such as number and measurement. Sunniva could not wait to get to school and was sorely disappointed if illness kept her away – school was an adventure and made her happy.

My youngest daughter Jenny, now 4, also started at the infant–toddler centre when she was very small; at 8 months. By this time I was married and running my own business in Reggio and had far fewer points when applying for a place. At this juncture I was able to appreciate the fairness of the place allocation system although my need was less second time round, but fortunately we got a place at our second choice school. Substantially I found very little changed in the 12 years since Sunniva started apart from the obvious advances in technology which made the displays and records even more attractive. I immediately felt very at home in such familiar surroundings.

At the end of Jenny's second year at the infant–toddler centre I sold my business and started working very much reduced hours as a free-lance interpreter for, among others, Reggio Children. I have now worked as an interpreter for a number of delegations and have had the opportunity to visit quite a few schools. While the interpreter's job is strictly to act as linguistic glue for the two sides of the exchange, as a parent I was frequently drawn into the discussion myself. This was further confirmation for me of the real open-endedness of the Reggio approach, the willingness to listen and learn from everyone and everything, the readiness to change and adapt, the desire to ascribe each person, regardless of his or her role, with an equally important potential for contribution.

Children who go to the infant–toddler centres are not automatically given places at the preschools and when it came to applying for a place at a preschool for Jenny, not only did we have very few points, but the demand for places had risen enormously since Sunniva's day. We ran the risk of having to enrol her at a state or private (mostly Church) preschool in order to continue her preschool education as it would have been unthinkable to interrupt it at this stage. I was very reluctant to have to choose an alternative with a completely different educational approach and was very relieved to be awarded a place at the last minute in a preschool which was in the process of being hastily cobbled together out of ex-council offices in an apartment block to meet the demand. At the party held for the opening of the school I asked how, given the importance lent to the environment in the children's learning process in the Reggio philosophy, was our children's experience going to be affected in a school that had none of the essential architectural features as defined by the Reggio approach: circularity, transparency, access to the outside from each classroom, the *piazza*, and so on. I was reassured by the answer I knew I was going to get and six months on into the experience can endorse its validity. Of all the schools, very few were purpose-built and some of the most rewarding experiences have been gleaned from all the staff and children and parents taking up the challenge presented by a non-ideal environment and getting the best out of it. Our school represents a considerable challenge and many new parents felt decidedly uneasy about it at the beginning of the year, also partly due to the decision by the staff to fill the school with work produced by the children over time. Until this policy was fully explained many parents complained about how anonymous and bare the environment was, but rather like after moving into a new home, even in this short time the school is beginning to look 'lived in' and, more importantly, by our children and *their* products.

I have been elected – after volunteering – to the management committee as a parent representative and hope to become instrumental in the growth and future of the school, particularly in areas that have particular pertinence to my own situation. When Sunniva started at her infant–toddler centre in 1984 we were the only family in the school with a second language and a foreign parent. Now, in Jenny's class there is a wide assortment of nationalities and first and second languages that reflect the increasing immigration into Reggio Emilia from many parts of Africa, Asia, Eastern Europe and the Middle East. I have been continually impressed by the ease with which the children from these families have settled into the Reggio schools and feel that, as it was in my case, this is due to the idea of difference being interpreted as an opportunity for increasing the resources available for the children to explore. Here again parents and family are actively encouraged to become involved; my father once put in an appearance at Sunniva's preschool in his full dress kilt and regalia!

Jenny will have another two years at the preschool and will start primary school just as Sunniva is leaving school altogether. I can only hope that the transition from preschool to state primary school will be as smooth for Jenny as it was for Sunniva. This was not due, however, to any formal or official policy but to the exceptional personal qualities of Sunniva's gifted primary school teachers and her luck in finding herself in their hands. Given the abyss dividing the Reggio local authority preschools from the state primary schools in terms of approach and quality, in the last year of preschool most of the parent get-togethers are taken up with discussing their children's future schooling with the kind of blind hope and fatalism normally associated with buying lottery tickets.

I have often been asked, and ask myself, what I feel Sunniva has gained from her preschool experience and what contribution it has made to her all-round development. It is a very subjective question and obviously I have no terms for any type of comparison. My feeling is, however, that as Loris Malaguzzi put it, she has been given an 'extra pocket' of resources to dip into as she wishes and that as result the world is as exciting and challenging a place for her now as when she was a small child.

6 Sam's invisible extra gear – a parent's view

Jenny Leask

My name is Jenny Leask and I'm the mother of Sam, aged 6. My first contact with the Reggio Emilia preschools was in 1986 when I stayed with Caroline Hunter and visited her elder daughter's infant–toddler centre, and later on her preschool. At that time I was teaching in Britain and I clearly remember the enormous impact the schools made on me – the work the children were doing, the wonderfully rich and stimulating visual environment, as well as a parent's evening which culminated in an informal supper washed down with Lambrusco sitting at long benches under the stars. It was all so different from anything I had experienced in (at that time) ten years of teaching experience in Britain. I returned home and thought about everything. Why did my classroom feel so much just a classroom compared to those I had seen in Reggio? Why did the children's work seem so different and sophisticated? How did all the delicate and beautiful treasures in the *atelier* remain intact despite the full use they were getting from the children? Why did my display seem to be just that, instead of the very full documentation of planning and work in progress that I'd seen in the infant–toddler centre and preschool that I'd visited?

In 1991 we came here to live and in February 1994 Sam was born. Despite my respect and admiration for everything I'd seen on my previous visits to Reggio, when the time came for me to return to work and Sam to be enrolled in an infant–toddler centre both Sam's father Andrea and I were very reluctant to consign our precious 7 month old first-born to the care of the municipality. Nevertheless we went ahead with our application and were duly informed that Sam had been offered a place at the Arcobaleno, our first choice, and that we should all go along for an initial interview with the teachers at the end of August. Promising ourselves that if we didn't like it we didn't have to take the place, along we went – not realizing how lucky we were to have been offered a place at all, let alone in our first choice! Entering the school for the first time, the impact of my first impressions of so many years before came flooding back as we looked around a light open space filled with examples of children's work (but this was August – why weren't the walls bare?), written panels illustrated with photos, plants, a mix of small chairs and antique furniture, *bric-à-brac*, tiny beautiful treasures, delicate old objects and instruments, photos and examples of work that had obviously been there for many years – the sort of domestic archaeological layering that takes place over time in all our homes.

Our first meeting was with the two full-time teachers who would be working with Sam's group, and the school cook who was introduced to us as a central figure in the life of the school. We sat together and the teachers asked us a series of very detailed questions about Sam and his habits and preferences. How did he behave when he was tired? How did he like being held? What did he like doing? What sort of character was he? What sort of routine did we have at home? What type of home life did we have – quiet and regulated, or full of comings and goings? All our answers were carefully noted down. We saw them again three weeks later as we entered his room, reproduced and displayed on the wall alongside his picture together with similar details and photos of all the other children in his group. A little biography of our boy! Twelve little biographies of these small individuals who were all at the start of their own journeys – we read them all avidly and started to see Sam as part of this little band of adventurers. Then we saw a list of all us parents – our names, dates and places of birth, our education and our professions – and it dawned on us that we were part of that group too, about to become part of the school.

Sam settled in very smoothly, helped by the staggered entry system which meant that five or six children started week by week. Parents were allowed to stay with the children as long as we and the teachers felt it was necessary. I look back at the mornings spent in Sam's room at Arcobaleno as a lovely time; watching him settling into an environment outside the home, watching him relating to the other children and his teachers. For Andrea and I there was the equal pleasure of getting to know his teachers and the other parents in such a relaxed setting. When I left Sam for the first time my short walk to the bar for a coffee was trailed by his wailing, and I felt immensely reassured when I returned and found him happily playing in his sunny room with the radio on after a trip to the kitchen to get a biscuit. After two weeks I returned to work and went to collect him at midday after his lunch, although he could have stayed until 4 o'clock or, by special arrangement, until 6.20. The teachers were always ready to talk and listen at the beginning and end of the day and there were daily running records showing what Sam had had for lunch, his bodily functions (riveting reading) and the activities the group had been involved in during the day. Alongside these records was an outline of the week's projected activities and very often advertisements and publicity for social and cultural events that were taking place in the town. Over the course of the year written panels appeared at both child and adult height in Sam's room documenting with words and photographs moments in the children's learning – observations of work in progress. These panels are incredibly affecting in their projection of your own or someone else's child as protagonists in their own learning. The readily available range of written information, the opportunity to talk with the endlessly patient teachers at the beginning and end of the day and the exchanges with other parents sitting in the garden while our children played made us feel very much part of the school. The building itself, with its light and welcoming spaces, and the kitchen (source of delicious smells of cooking and fresh coffee) with its door always open to children and parents alike, played a very important role in our feeling of belonging. We felt so proud and privileged to be part of such a place and process.

As parents in this setting we were initially quite surprised to realize that the teachers seemed to value our part in our child's learning. The feeling of reciprocal respect and affection between the adults in the school, the children and the parents meant that we were more than willing to reciprocate in terms of attendance at meetings and participation in school activities. We could be involved on a practical level by volunteering our experience or skills to help construct or repair indoor and outdoor equipment, or we could become involved with the planning of outings and celebrations such as end of year parties, special days for particular groups such as grandparents, summer solstice festivities, or the grape or chestnut harvest. As a jazz pianist, Andrea is often in demand on these occasions. On an administrative level, parents may be involved in the running of the school through elected membership of school councils and parent's committees who organize meetings and discussions themed around cultural concerns such as television, diet or divorce. Parents are encouraged to be involved in meetings held by the schools to discuss policy concerns and educational matters.

Another arena for information and exchange is the parent's meetings, held three of four times a term with varying formats and illustrated with slides and/or videos as well as the children's work. There may be a whole class meeting about a theme that the class has been exploring together over a period of time, or sometimes the meetings may be for small groups of parents looking at activities their children have been engaged in together. In either case the meetings rarely start before 9 p.m. and always go on until well after midnight. I am always most impressed when I arrive somewhat blearily the next morning to see the teachers looking as cheerful as ever.

A very special end of year treat at the end of Sam's first year at Arcobaleno was the presentation of a large yearbook full of photos and observations of Sam. This beautifully presented book went back to the school to be added to at the end of every school year and is still taken out and looked at regularly at home. The yearbook changes and evolves as the children move up through their preschools, with more examples of the children's work being included as well as a portfolio of artwork.

After a very happy three years at Arcobaleno the time came for Sam to transfer to Anna Frank, his preschool. The exchange was handled very sensitively with the teachers ready to talk about any anxieties we, the parents, might have been feeling about the changeover, and having the chance to talk to the other parents was a real help as well. The children needed no such reassurance!

We were given the opportunity to look at the preschools in our area after school hours and we decided to apply to Anna Frank. Lucky again, our application was accepted and we again found ourselves meeting with Sam's new teachers individually before the beginning of the school year. Our impressions of his new school were thankfully familiar: a warm, welcoming, multilayered environment, great attention paid by his teachers to Sam's character and preferences and a tea party in the school garden the week before term started to welcome the group of parents and children. Throughout Sam's time at Anna Frank the same attention to detail that was evident at Arcobaleno has been apparent. The parent's meetings are always illustrated by slides or videos of the children involved in work in progress, projects or outings. Statements of intent for the week, the term and the year are pinned up in the class-room alongside a daily plan and a daily diary showing how the plan may have changed course or been adapted according to what the children have come up with. Examples of the children's work are up on the walls together with written explanations of the starting point, fragments of dialogue, photos of the children at work and their own explanations of what they are doing. As a parent I find that all these various types of documentation provide a vivid, clear, exciting and at times very moving understanding of, and access to, Sam's life in school, as well as opening my eyes to the idea of children as navigators in their own learning. The Anna Frank School also has its history and beginnings clearly visible alongside its present in the form of photos, writings, panels, models, structures and paintings. Delicious smells welcome the visitor, beautiful objects delight the eye, the spaces flow from one to another and the adults in the school, the children and the parents seem to hold each other in mutual affection and respect. I am so pleased that Sam has been part of this experience, and I'm so pleased that we have too.

Sam is now coming to the end of his time at Anna Frank and in September 2000 will embark on the next stage of his educational journey at state elementary school. I think that our experiences as parents at Arcobaleno and Anna Frank have profoundly changed our ideas and expectations regarding children, adults and parents learning together in the community of school. The schools' approach to children as competent capable individuals seems to result in a genuine sense of collectivity between the adults in the school, the children and the parents. I think it was this which really confounded our own expectations of school as being a place where children went to be taught, teachers worked alone and parents waited at the gate. I feel sure that Sam's experiences here in the Reggio schools will always stay with him, and us, as a kind of invisible extra gear.

Over the last six years I've been lucky enough to act as an interpreter for some of the many delegations that visit the city and the schools of Reggio, and sometimes I have attended group sessions from these delegations as a parent. In both situations I find myself looking at the schools with a huge sense of pride, almost as if I were a real *reggiana* (citizen of Reggio). Perhaps this sense of place and belonging to a community based on openness, trust and respect has been their great gift to me as a foreign mother, and to us as a family.

Special needs or special rights?

Sylvia Phillips

As we entered Reggio Emilia at the beginning of the Study Week, we passed the grand, classical façade of the opera house. Hanging from each column were long white banners with writing on them – not an unusual sight. Theatres the world over often have such banners advertising current productions, with quotations from the opera or from critical reviews. What was remarkable was that when we went closer, we saw that these were quotations from local children, aged 4–6, presenting their views on the war in Kosovo, with no adult comment or 'explanations'. While this was not the first time I have read such thoughts, never have I seen them so grandly and publicly displayed.

This, for me, captured two essential principles of the Reggio Emilia approach – the recognition and valuing of children's views as members of society, and the significance of involving the whole community. Fundamental to the Reggio system are the principles of acknowledging children's rights, valuing childhood and accepting that responsibility for educating even the youngest of children rests within the community or municipality.

The philosophy and pedagogy of the Reggio approach is one of the most clearly articulated for early years education. It is not static but always developing, with the directors, pedagogists and teachers constantly refining and modifying their approaches to educating young children. They place a high value on the language and terms used to describe their educational processes. Thus, the Reggio Emilia preschools have eschewed the Italian term usually used for schools for children aged 3–6 (*scuo'la materna*), preferring the term *scuola d'infanzia* because this clearly puts the focus on the child. They admitted that currently they are even rethinking this, having discovered that the origin of the meaning of 'infant' is 'without language', and clearly, therefore, at odds with their philosophy of appreciating the 'hundred languages' of children. This care and attention to interpreting and using language is also evident in their preference for the term 'special rights' rather than (in rejecting 'handicapped') adopting 'special needs' or 'special educational needs', the descriptions used in many countries, including the UK. It is interesting, therefore, to explore the Reggio Emilia approach to children with 'special rights' or 'special needs' within the Italian context and in relation to our current thinking and experiences in the UK.

Italy was one of the first countries in Europe (along with Norway) to introduce legislation for the 'integration' of Children with Special Rights into mainstream schools. The process began in 1971 and the law of 1977 determined that: 'All children with handicaps, regardless of the nature and seriousness of their handicaps, are to be integrated in normal mainstream school classes' (Menegoi-Buzzi 1999: 18). The legislation also provides for specialist support teachers to be available. The law applies not only to state schools catering for those within compulsory schooling (6–14 years) but also, since the 1980s, to state kindergarten schools (*scuo'la materna*). Just over 90 per cent of all 3–5-year-olds in Italy attend preschools, with the highest proportions being found in the more affluent northern cities. Forty-seven per cent are in state nurseries, with the remainder being in municipal and private (religious and non-religious) establishments. In Reggio Emilia, which is part municipal-funded, fees are payable, but there is a sliding scale related to parents' income. Children with special rights are given priority, we were told, although the criteria for being identified as having special rights were not published at that time.

Despite the early Italian legislation on integration, many children with profound, multiple learning and physical disabilities receive support and therapies within a community health system for some or all of each day. Pijl and Meijer (1991) report that Italy defines 1.7 per cent of its school population as having special needs (about the same percentage as those placed in special schools in England when the Warnock Report (DES 1978) was published). In 1991 they reported that 0.2 per cent were in mainstream schools, 0.2 per cent in totally segregated special provision and a further 1.3 per cent who were 'hard to integrate' were placed in special units or classes in mainstream schools, often being taught in segregated situations. In general the incidence of inclusion/integration is higher in the North of Italy than the South (Menegoi-Buzzi 1998).

Until very recently, the term 'handicapped' has been used in Italy to describe children with special needs (*bambini handicappa're*) and it is interesting to note that several of the teachers in the preschools we visited still used this term. This draws attention to a major difference between the wider definition of special educational needs which we have come to use in England since the 1981 Education Act and the definition used in most European countries which focuses on severe and complex intellectual difficulties and physical disabilities. It is very important to appreciate this distinction, because it can affect how we interpret the (general) Italian, and more specifically the Reggio Emilia approach, to integration and/or inclusion. Vianello and Moniga (1995: 42) point to the necessity to note the different use, 'since from these labels derive teaching policies'. Only children with a severe learning difficulty (IQ less than 65) or a severe physical disability, sensory impairment or emotional disturbance are included in the Italian definition.

Although several years have passed since the UK 1981 Education Act, stating that children with special educational needs should wherever possible be educated in 'ordinary schools', was implemented, both the Green Paper on special educational needs (DfEE 1997) and *Meeting Special Educational Needs: A Programme for Action* (DfEE 1998) are still only promoting inclusion, 'where parents want it and appropriate support can be provided' (DfEE 1998: 23). There is an emphasis on building 'a more inclusive education system' (DfEE 1998: 22) rather than compelling mainstream schools to become inclusive. Nevertheless, it is now the case in England that children with statements for severe and complex difficulties are increasingly being educated in mainstream schools with their peers. As many writers have pointed out, this does not mean that the schools have necessarily become 'inclusive'. Many practices still emphasize 'difference' from 'normal children' and many reproduce segregation within the mainstream setting.

Clark *et al.* (1995) have argued that three paradigms dominate research into special education and provide frameworks for analysing inclusive practices. These paradigms are 'the psycho-medical', with its emphasis on individual children and deficits, the 'socio-political', which highlights how structural inequalities at a macro-social level are reproduced in institutional form, and the 'organizational paradigm' which focuses on perceived inadequacies in the current curriculum and organization of mainstream schools. As they point out, this latter paradigm is currently the view most widely held in the UK and, of course, finds political favour because it is closely associated with research into schools' effectiveness and school improvement. The basic tenet is that schools should develop strategies 'which enhance educational benefits and opportunities for all pupils rather than targeting particular "special" populations', (Clark *et al.* 1995: 79). This approach is strongly argued for by Ainscow (1994, 1995) who suggests that schools should adopt a problem solving approach to meet the diversity of their populations, foster more collaborative work and ensure the involvement of staff in planning, monitoring and evaluating their work. Clark *et al.* (1995: 81) point to some uneasiness about the 'apparently absolutist position that lurks beneath the

surface' of the organizational paradigm. The advocates of the organizational approach imply that few, if any, schools already have inclusive
practices and that they must adopt the 'problem-solving, collaborative,
reflective model' if they are to become 'inclusive'. Such an assertion
pathologizes schools which do not adopt this approach and also importantly gives rise to other concerns 'as to whose voices are heard and
whose silenced by this new paradigm' (Clark *et al.* 1995: 81).

It is also important to remember that critics of inclusive education in
the UK are considering a much wider range of special educational needs
(about 20 per cent of the school population) than is defined in Italy. The
UK definition includes that very large number of children who under-
achieve and experience temporary or long-term learning difficulties. The
need for a broad and differentiated curriculum to meet a range of different learning styles has long been accepted. A more radical shift in the
organization of some schools is sought to provide education that is more
comprehensive. Booth (2000: 78) emphasizes that inclusion must be
about 'giving learners an equality of regard irrespective of their background, gender, ethnicity, sexuality, disability or attainment'.

I endorse this definition and, clearly, a chapter on inclusion *per se*
would have to address these issues. In addition, it would have to enter
the debate on terminology about inclusion and integration. This chapter,
however, focuses more narrowly on how Reggio preschools provide
equality of opportunity for children with disabilities. Of particular relevance in Booth's statement is the phrase 'equality of regard'. Having
regard to children (which to me implies both respect and hearing, or
taking heed of, their voices) is evident in Reggio preschools. The issue
concerns the extent to which this includes *all* children.

In considering the Reggio approach it might be useful to see whether
using the individual child/psycho-medical and the curriculum/organiza-
tional paradigms throws light on provision for children with disabilities.
Concern about children and individuals and for developing an early
years' curriculum are central to Reggio schools. The Reggio pedagogy
does, in fact, demonstrate the problem in trying to distinguish discrete
paradigms and naively suggesting a shift from the former to the latter.

It is possible to construe the Reggio approach as one which upholds
the individual or psycho-medical paradigm. Italian law mandates redu-
cing class size (to no more than 20 children if one of them has a disability) and providing a specialist support teacher (*insegnante di sostegno*) to
support a child with a disability (at least one such teacher to four children with a disability). The ratio can be 1:1 depending on the severity of
the disability. Such practices, like our own, could be seen to be institu-
tionalizing the notion of 'difference'. Nevertheless, there is evidence
(internationally) to suggest that some children with severe disabilities do
require specialist (that is, different) kinds of teaching or levels of adult

intervention if they are to make progress. The debate should focus on how this support is used in ways which encourage maximum independence, achievement, socialization and active participation in learning, rather than necessarily view 'support' as a reflection on the inadequacy of a curriculum or mainstream teachers to meet diversity. Nevertheless, the curriculum should still be re-examined to maximize the learning and achievements of as many pupils as possible.

The 'inclusiveness' of a school is often judged on whether it simply 'admits' a child with a disability and permits participation (with support) rather than adjusting the curriculum and ways in which the teachers work. It is worth looking, therefore, at the Reggio curriculum/organization from this perspective. Talking to others during the Study Week, we discerned no apparent change in ways of working to ensure that the schools met the needs of children with special rights. As mentioned earlier, several teachers still described them as 'handicapped'. A major question therefore must be: 'Is the Reggio approach *itself* "inclusive"?' I would argue and hope to demonstrate that it is.

In her opening talk, Carla Rinaldi described the significance of the 'listening pedagogy' of Reggio. This involves not only listening to what children say and 'hearing' (interpreting) their understandings, but also observing and 'hearing' their hundred languages through all forms of expression. Surely, this is a fundamental right of *all* children, and such pedagogy means that children's views are respected. This gives a 'voice' also to children with a disability. Where teachers act in response to what children have said, then this shows regard. When the children had talked about their views on the war in Kosovo and what they had seen on television, the teachers did not merely document and display their views. They used them to discuss and explore feelings and responses, helping them to construct, share and understand their own views and those of others.

Loris Malaguzzi's emphasis is on the child's 'hundred ways of thinking, of playing, of speaking' and the need to recognize diversity, not quell it, as society and schools ('they', in his poem) so often do:

They tell the child:
to think without hands
to do without head
and
They tell the child:
that work and play
reality and fantasy
science and imagination
sky and earth
reason and dream

are things
that do not belong together.

(Malaguzzi 1996: i)

Underpinning the Reggio approach is the strong emphasis on creativity. Each preschool has an artist (*atelierista*) and well-resourced studio (*atelier*) where children work with the *atelierista* in groups on a variety of projects. The curriculum emphasizes art, drawing, music, play and an appreciation of their history and culture. It therefore provides a wide range of avenues for learning which are less likely to exclude children with language/cognitive difficulties than a more 'academically-focused' curriculum.

However, their use of creativity should not be seen solely as the development of artistic skills themselves, important as they are, but rather as the means of developing skills of enquiry, of thinking, observing, understanding and making choices. This environment produces what Carl Rogers (1969) called 'freedom to learn'. The teachers facilitate children's discovery, helping them to enjoy learning – and, through observation and interpretation of what the children do, further develop and extend children's learning and spirit of enquiry.

All the schools visited were visually attractive, showing imaginative use of light, shade and colour. As UK educators visiting in 1999, we were impressed by the creativity of the children and their opportunities to delight in exploring their environment. There is a clear commitment to an early years pedagogy which does not prescribe a curriculum geared towards achievement in literacy and numeracy. The 4–6-year-olds in the *scuola d'infanzia* would, we reminded ourselves, be involved in baseline assessments, literacy and numeracy hours in England. While many could point to nursery schools and Early Excellence Centres in the UK where there *is* an emphasis on play and creativity similar to that in Reggio Emilia, many also shared a concern that there is a:

> new and rather dangerous tendency to let *that* curriculum [the National Curriculum] press down upon the provision for even the youngest children . . . and that since [politicians] are becoming more and more convinced that early education matters, then it should be a version of that which they deem appropriate for older children.
>
> (Gammage 1992: 3)

In view of such concerns, the early years educators valued the celebration of childhood encountered in the Reggio Emilia curriculum.

The recent report *All Our Futures: Creativity, Culture and Education* (DfEE 1999) proposes a wide view of creativity, similar to that taken in Reggio (although it deliberately places less emphasis on the arts). Creativity, in that publication, is defined as: 'Imaginative activity fashioned so as to produce outcomes that are both original and of value' (p. 29). *All Our Futures* has been welcomed as an attempt not only to restore breadth to the curriculum, but also as a means of extending horizons, development and invention across all fields of life. The report emphasizes that *everyone* can be creative, and that 'Creative abilities are developed through practical application: by being engaged in the processes of creative thought production' (p. 32).

The emphasis on learning how to learn, on active discovery and a sensory curriculum is very evident in the Reggio preschools. There we saw children making clay sculptures of their own heads, by first observing and examining their faces and features in mirrors and drawing their self-portraits (as cartoons or drafts) before modelling the clay. Their results varied, showing facial expressions and attention to detail which exceeded the usual products of children the same age who have not participated in similar staged processes. Active learning situations and multi-sensory teaching have been shown to benefit many children with special educational needs. A highly visual and sensory curriculum stimulates learning through several modes, so that children may build on their strengths. The Reggio curriculum therefore seems highly appropriate for many children with disabilities provided they have 'enabled' access.

The fact that there is not an emphasis on acquiring basic literacy and numeracy skills within the Reggio preschools may also be to the advantage of young children who, for whatever reason, may experience developmental delay. While in a stimulating, supportive environment, their general cognitive, language and social development may be fostered so that they also, in common with their peers, learn 'how to learn'. All too often, demands for academic attainments in literacy and numeracy in the early years can lead to low achievement and experience of failure either then or later. The achievement 'gaps' between children with learning difficulties and their peers soon widens and, as the Green Paper *Excellence for* All *Children* suggests: 'When educational failure becomes entrenched, pupils can move from demoralisation to disruptive behaviour and truancy' (DfEE 1997: 12–13).

Herein, of course, lies one of the main dilemmas of teaching in the special educational needs field. Norwich (1993) points to the many dilemmas in special educational needs work. Early specialist intervention can be a means of pointing to great difference from 'other' children (normal children? able children?), leading to stigma and a pathological approach to disability. However, lack of specific intervention can equally lead to a widening of discrepancies in learning and prevent a child with a disability from achieving. What is important in the Italian system is that individualized targets can be set without measuring success against normative standards at too early a stage of education. Most educationalists agree on the importance of early identification and intervention for children with special needs. An integrated multiprofessional approach by health services, social services and educators is adopted in both Italy and the UK, although it was not clear how this operates in the Reggio schools. I have, however, seen evidence of successful multiprofessional cooperation elsewhere in Italy, particularly in early years education.

Children with special rights in the Reggio preschools are supported by specialist support teachers (many of whom currently hold higher qualifications than those employed as class teachers). Italian support teachers participate in the weekly in-service sessions which are built into all the teachers' timetables. (This is true for all Italian primary and pre-primary state schools as well as those in Reggio Emilia.) However, support teachers hold a generic qualification in supporting children with disabilities and may therefore not be able to deliver specialist intervention programmes to children with very severe difficulties in, say, language development or those who have a severe hearing loss. Moreover, in the preschools visited support teachers did not seem to have adopted an advisory or consultancy role to work collaboratively with class teachers in planning appropriate work. For the most part, children with disabilities joined in the main curriculum but did not seem to have additional individualized programmes or individualized targets within the curriculum. There appears to be no evaluation as to how these preschool experiences affect their future attainment and development. It is difficult to discern, therefore, the extent to which their *individual* learning needs are met although it is clear that they are able to be present in all activities undertaken by their peers.

The specialist teachers were very aware of the need to develop both social relationships and independence. In establishing the principles of the Reggio approach, Malaguzzi emphasized the importance of social interactions and of the value of working and negotiating within groups: 'Such negotiation and communication produces more exchange than in adult–child interaction' (Edwards *et al.* 1993: 11).

Developing relationships is also a foundation for citizenship, and the large *piazzas* in the Reggio preschools are seen as important in developing a community and as a microcosm of society paralleling the city *piazzas*. They are large, open places where children wander, meet each other, play imaginatively, meet children from other age groups and develop socially. Daniela (aged 4) who has cerebral palsy and learning difficulties, was pushed (in her wheelchair) by her support teacher, to join different groups in the *piazza*. For a time she appeared 'on the fringe' of a group of three girls who were 'dressing up' in dresses and cloaks and talking to each other. The support teacher did not intervene. After a few minutes, one of the girls selected a long piece of lace, draped it round Daniela's shoulders, and told her she was beautiful (*bellissima*). This was, in fact, the only interaction with peers experienced by Daniela that morning. Freedom to make initiatives and choices may mean some isolation unless adults intervene, and little adult intervention was observed in the *piazza*. It is impossible to make any judgements about the extent to which social interactions and relationships are engineered based on a half-day visit and I do not know how typical this observation is.

At another school, however, Paulo (aged 5) was taken from his wheelchair early in the morning and joined the class both in listening to a story and the following session where the children made choices about their next activity. When the children moved into small groups, he sat alone for some time, before painstakingly crawling to a chair at a low table. His support teacher then 'moved in' to help him sit. This appeared to be a good example of encouraging independence and effort to achieve what is possible, while providing support when the challenge is beyond (current) capacity. Paulo then participated in an activity involving matching cards/pictures with two other children. This involved some scaffolding of language from the support teacher. All three children worked cooperatively while the teacher made notes on her observations of what they said and did. This careful documentation, data collection and analysis is remarked on elsewhere in this book as a characteristic of the Reggio approach. It was unclear as to how the notes were used to monitor the progress of individual children and set targets, but such documentation is certainly used in teachers' in-service sessions to raise their understanding of children's learning and help plan projects. It is interesting to note that Ainscow (1995) identifies one of the characteristic conditions that facilitate schools becoming more inclusive as 'teacher-enquiry and reflection'. He draws attention to the importance of encouraging staff to be involved in the processes of data collection and analysis, and using this information to inform decision making. In the same chapter, he also says inclusive/effective schools would: 'see professional learning as essential to improvement; allocate time for staff development activities' (Ainscow 1995: 76). Both characteristics are integral to the Reggio approach.

Although the preschools do not have an emphasis on teaching literacy and numeracy, they do not, of course prevent it. Indeed, because of the amount of documentation that takes place (through both writing and photographic records), children observe adult models actively engaged in writing more than in English preschools. They are also particularly encouraged to communicate with each other and have pigeon-holes/cubby-holes where they can send each other 'communications' in the form of small drawings and 'messages' (words or letter-like marks). I have observed this as a significant feature in several *scuola materna* in Italy as well as in English nurseries and Reception classes. Developing writing and reading skills are seen as 'emergent' processes, as are numeracy skills. They are not, however, seen as the *core purposes* of the

Reggio preschools, and children's progress is not therefore judged in relation to their use/development of writing or numeracy.

It is clear, therefore, that the preschools of Reggio have much to offer children with special educational needs. The choice of the term 'special rights' rather than 'special needs' is consistent with their approach to *valuing* all children rather than seeing them as 'inadequate adults' and perceiving deficits. Children's insights are not only acknowledged, but are also the subject of marvel and advancing adult knowledge and understanding. It follows that children's strengths are considered, rather than their deficits and weaknesses. The preschools in Reggio Emilia recognized children's rights long before the publication of the United Nations' Convention on the Rights of the Child in 1989. They established children's rights to be heard and have their views considered, and have published some of their children's views on 'rights'. These do not differ from the words of children of the same age in other countries when asked for similar statements (they include statements about whether parents have a right to get angry with you 'when you're naughty' and a child's right not to eat things they 'don't like'). The Reggio Emilia approach visibly empowers children and promotes their rights as described within the United Nations' Convention.

The United Nations' Convention on the Rights of the Child contains 54 articles defining the range of children's rights, grouped under the four categories of:

1. prevention (largely related to health);
2. provision (including access to education and with some specific reference to the rights of children with disabilities) (Article 23);
3. protection (from neglect and exploitation); and
4. participation (including the right to express their views and 'be heard').

This latter is particularly important for people with a disability. Article 29 emphasizes that education (a right under Article 28) shall be directed to: 'The development of the child's personality, talents and mental and physical abilities to their fullest potential'; and Article 31 says that: 'States Parties shall respect and promote the right of the child to participate fully in cultural and artistic life and shall encourage the provision of appropriate and equal opportunities for cultural, artistic, recreational and leisure activity'. The Reggio preschools clearly also promote this right. In particular, Article 13 offers children the right to: 'Freedom of expression; this right shall include freedom to seek, receive and impart information and ideas of all kinds, regardless of frontiers, either orally, in writing or in print, in the form of art, or through any other media of the child's choice'.

Reggio Emilia preschools guard these rights jealously: they are fundamental to their philosophy. Is there, then, any need to use the word 'special'? What additional or different rights are required by children with disabilities or 'needs'? While the term 'rights' put the Reggio approach into a rights discourse rather than deficit one, it is arguable that it is the word 'special' which still maintains the deficit/medical paradigm as it differentiates them from other children. In any country which has ratified the Convention, surely the only question is *how* to ensure all children have these rights? It may be that particular methods have to be sought or required for some children, implying additional or different support (long-term or temporary). This line of reasoning is reminiscent of Warnock's recommendations (DES 1978) referring to the goals of education rather than rights – that they are 'the same for all children' but the means of attaining them may differ. One of the problems here lies in the question as to whether this can be used to segregate and/or make the means or pathway to them so different that it denies children their fundamental rights to equality. 'Special' rights may similarly promote a pathological approach. In trying to identify the 'special rights' of Reggio's children, the only ones to emerge are:

- Some children (those with a disability) are given priority in allocating places within a preschool. This is significant, given that not all the local children can attend. It is a form of positive discrimination which protects them, *at least*, from exclusion.
- That such children (by Italian law) have a right to a 'support teacher' on a ratio of at least 1:4.
- That they have the right to be taught in classes of no more than 20 (by Italian law).

Which children have 'special rights'? These appeared to be children with disabilities, particularly those experiencing physical disabilities, although no overt criteria were made known to us. While such children are less than 2 per cent of the school population, we saw very few in the preschools and some said they had no children with special rights. We wondered how parents learn of their children's 'special rights' to priority places? Do the majority send their children to state provision? We saw no children with severe autism, for example, and wondered where these children's needs/rights are met. Are they in 'health' provision, which does not necessarily include qualified teachers? Also remarkable was that one of the schools which has only been built seven years, was designed on two storeys, but with no access for children with impaired mobility/in wheelchairs. A response to a question about this was 'You can't think of everything' (defending themselves or the architects?) – which seemed at odds not only with the concept of 'special rights' but also a country which has had legislation about 'integrated schooling' for over 20 years (15 in the case of preschools). Assurance was given that plans for new buildings have ensured access. While our attention was drawn to the wide, open spaces available in the *piazzas* and many class-rooms, access within the *ateliers* was often more limited, and some of the very small within-class *ateliers* could not provide access for children in wheelchairs. These issues need to be addressed. Similarly, not all materials, books etc. were within the reach of children in wheelchairs.

It is important, however, not to equate inclusivity and the notion of 'barrier-free' schools simply with physical access. It is the openness and appropriateness of the curriculum (including its organization, teaching and learning styles) and the climate of the school which make a school 'inclusive'. In all these respects, Reggio Emilia appears to meet the 'rights' of all children. Some may have particular and complex learning 'needs' where it is less clear that their individual difficulties are identified and met. No evaluation is available yet. This appears strange in view of the emphasis on recording. However, the focus of documentation has, certainly until now, been more about 'how children learn' rather than how any individual child might learn.

One major area which I am sure will be addressed shortly is to make the inclusion, involvement and contributions of children with disabilities more transparent. Documentation about the Reggio experience and philosophy is displayed on the walls of both the infant–toddler centres and the preschools. It provides constant reminders to staff, parents, children and visitors of the learning and achievements of children and the philosophy and practices of the Reggio pedagogy. None of the displays and photographs we saw, however, included images of children with 'special rights'. While tokenism should be avoided, there are ways of promoting positive images which not only enhance the self-image of children with disabilities (and their parents) but also recognize and celebrate diversity. This does not make them 'special' but it is their *right*. This is part of equality of opportunity. *Not* being represented can be seen as exclusion.

I wondered also about how the 'non-disabled' perceive the children with a disability. I saw no statement about this and indeed, would agree that direct questioning is further likely to draw attention and give *significance* to 'difference'. Overall, I was pleased to see no formal statements about children's perceptions on disability. However, as Vlachou (1997) has shown, such perceptions may hold lessons for teachers.

This chapter has highlighted the problems of finding terms to describe children with learning difficulties and/or disabilities. While many prefer an emphasis on 'rights' rather than 'needs' what essentially is important is the rights of *all* children to participate *fully in, and benefit from*, educational experiences and play a full part in society. There is no simple solution to ensuring that all children can do this without using terms which in themselves point to individual and group differences. I have, within this chapter, used the word 'disability' as if it somehow distinguished some children from others, but also as a means of *not* using only the terms 'special needs' or 'special rights'. In all cases, however, as in Reggio Emilia, the word 'children' comes first.

Finally, no chapter about 'special educational needs' or disability can be complete without considering parents' rights. Parental involvement is given a high priority in the Reggio preschools and parents are actively involved not so much as helpers and educators within the schools, but within Reggio administration and policymaking. They have a clear 'voice' in the development of the preschools. Many are also involved as 'friends of Reggio Children' and those we met articulate the philosophy clearly and understand its practices. They verify how much their children have benefited from attending Reggio preschools. Several were, however, very critical of the elementary schools their children would enter (or had entered) at the age of 6, seeing them as formal, academic institutions with very traditional curricula. One parent quoted Malaguzzi, saying that he hoped that the Reggio Emilia preschools had given their children 'extra pocket'. He hoped that children's self-confidence in themselves as learners, their self-esteem and enjoyment of learning would be so strong that it could sustain them even through less challenging and supportive educational experiences. Our parent-guide, describing her own daughter's elementary school years, firmly believed that the Reggio experience and the 'extra pocket' was what had helped her to persevere into secondary education (see Chapter 5).

We did not meet any parents of children with disabilities, but we can hope that the Reggio experience also provides each of them with an 'extra pocket' for the future.

References

Ainscow, M. (1994) *Special needs in the Classroom: A Teacher Education Guide.* London: Jessica Kingsley/UNESCO.

Ainscow, M. (1995) Special needs through school improvement: school improvement through special needs, in C. Clark, A. Dyson and A. Millward (eds) *Towards Inclusive Schools?* pp. 62–77. London: David Fulton.

Booth, T. (2000) Inclusion and exclusion policy in England: who controls the agenda?, in F. Armstrong, D. Armstrong and L. Barton (eds) *Inclusive Education: Policy, Contexts and Comparative Perspectives,* pp. 78–89. London: David Fulton.

Clark, C., Dyson, A., Millward, A. and Skidmore, D. (1995) Dialectical analysis, special needs and schools as organisations, in C. Clark, A. Dyson and A. Millward (eds) *Towards Inclusive Schools?* pp. 78–95. London: David Fulton.

DES (Department of Education and Science) (1978) *Special Educational Needs* (The Warnock Report). London: HMSO.

DfEE (Department for Education and Employment) (1997) *Excellence for All Children: Meeting Special Educational Needs.* London: HMSO.

DfEE (Department for Education and Employment) (1998) *Meeting Special Educational Needs: A Programme for Action.* London: DfEE Publications.

DfEE (Department for Education and Employment) (1999) *All Our Futures: Creativity, Culture and Education.* London: DfEE Publications.

Edwards, C., Gandini, L. and Forman, G. (eds) (1993) *The Hundred Languages of Children – The Reggio Emilia Approach to Early Childhood Education.* Norwood, NJ: Ablex.

Gammage, P. (1992) *Standing Conference on Education and Training of Teachers, Occasional Paper 1 – Quality: The Tension Between Content and Process.* Nottingham: University of Nottingham.

Malaguzzi, L. (1996) *The Hundred Languages of Children* (exhibition catalogue). Reggio Emilia: Reggio Children.

Menegoi-Buzzi, I. (1998) Integration in Italy. Lecture at transnational course, Desenzano, Italy, November.

Menegoi-Buzzi, I. (1999) A critical view of integration in Italy, in M. Chaltin, I. Menegoi-Buzzi, S. Phillips and N. Sylvestre (eds) *Integrating Children With Specific Educational Needs (Handicapped) in Ordinary Schools: Case Studies in Europe,* pp. 18–22. Milan: IRRSAE, Lombardia.

Norwich, B. (1993) Ideological dilemmas in SEN. *Oxford Review of Education,* 19(4): 527–46.

Pijl, S.J. and Meijer, C.J.W. (1991) Does integration count for much? An analysis of the practices of integration in eight countries, *European Journal of Special Needs Education,* 6(2): 100–11.

Rogers, C.R. (1969) *Freedom to Learn.* Columbus, OH: Charles E. Merrill Publishing.

Vianello, R. and Moniga, S. (1995) Special education in Italy: integration of people with disabilities and the education of the teachers, in P. Mittler and P. Daunt (eds) *Teacher Education for Special Needs in Europe,* pp. 53–63. London: Cassell.

Vlachou, A.D. (1997) *Struggles for Inclusive Education.* Buckingham: Open University Press.

A question of inclusion

Angela Nurse

> The fact that the rights of children are recognized as the rights of all children is a sign of a more accomplished humanity.
>
> (Reggio Children 1995: i)

Introduction

I returned hurriedly from my visit to Reggio Emilia, full of the powerful images I had seen and the discussions we had had, to see a production of the medieval miracle play *Everyman* staged in the magnificent chapel at the Royal Naval College in Greenwich. My young daughter was playing in the orchestra. The juxtaposition of this event with the powerful experience of visiting Reggio Emilia, as well as reflecting on my own child's infancy and adolescence, clarified and reaffirmed my thinking, not only about the visit, but also about my beliefs concerning early childhood education and care, and personal growth within a British, or more fundamentally, an English context. It also highlighted the importance of working together to produce something of beauty and worth, reaffirming the significance of group experience which has all but disappeared in the cult of 'individuality'.

The educators at Reggio Emilia were insistent that what we saw during our study visit was very much set in a context particular to this area and Italian culture. Although they were quick to allude to the part played by other traditions and philosophies (for example, traditional British nursery practice, High/Scope and Vygotsky) they impressed upon us throughout the week that the 'Reggio experience' could not be pulled up *in toto* and transplanted into another country and culture. Common strands about the nature of childhood could be transferred, but these needed to be set into an appropriate context, meaningful to the children and the community into which they were translated.

With this firmly in mind, this chapter includes general reflections on the approach to early childhood education in the Reggio Emilia preschools, leading into a discussion of the term 'inclusion'. This specifically addresses special needs, special educational needs and inclusion but with a broader perspective than a medically based definition of disability or illness. The term is also beginning to take on the dimension of 'social' inclusion for those on the margins of our society. The aim is to reveal how, or if, these needs are manifested and supported within the Reggio system.

Setting the context

Reggio Emilia, in the more prosperous northern part of Italy, close to the heart of Europe, has had a stable and relatively settled history since the ravages of extreme political factions and the Second World War. Its residents concede this, pointing out that it is only recently that the population of the town has begun to rise and alter with the arrival of immigrants from North Africa and refugees from the East. It is a beautiful town, secure in its recent history and proud of the decisions its people have taken to ensure that democracy thrives and is valued. Their commitment to children not only rests on a shared and stated philosophy that children are the responsibility of the whole community but also on the theory that by giving children a strong voice, enabling them to make decisions, to question and so to take control of their own learning, they will safeguard the future of democracy. The consistency of provision and practice within the Reggio Emilia group of nurseries is not matched by all the nurseries in this region nor throughout Italy. Penn (1997) has described others which offer a variable, sometimes less satisfying, régime for young children. Not every child within Reggio Emilia can have a place within these preschools and fees are charged on a sliding scale. Admissions are carefully considered using a strict set of criteria. It is interesting to see if, and then how, these contribute to prioritizing the admission of children with special needs.

The nurseries are beautiful places, another reflection of the emphasis placed on design and the visual arts which is a cultural priority for many Italians. Unlike so many of the spaces assigned to young children in the UK (and elsewhere), these are purpose-built or redesigned by architects to fit their new purpose. Old buildings are altered, after long discussions with all involved, but the best features are retained and enhanced: stone floors and sweeping staircases, for example. Knowledge, and perhaps memories, of the precious moments of childhood are recognized in the creation of hidden places where children can go to imagine and converse secretly with favoured friends. The nurseries are light and spacious. Natural materials are used to enhance the visual perspectives of the nursery as well as being there to touch, to smell and to capture the transitory sounds of natural mobiles fluttering in the breeze. It is a space devoid of the bright colours and fading sugar paper seen in some of our provision. Yet it provides a pale backdrop which enhances the colours of the natural and found objects with which the children work and enriches the intensity of colour in the children's creations. Children's work, models in clay, their drawings and comments, are preserved and carefully displayed. Materials are there to be selected by the children. Staff provide a range, far more extensive and hazardous than would be acceptable in the UK, where there is an insistent emphasis on health and safety. This enables children to deal themselves with more dangerous aspects of their environment. For example, there are trays of small beads and pieces of broken coloured glass for mosaics. In context, however, the educators ensure that children know how to handle these objects safely, using tweezers and protective gloves for example. The kitchen and dining rooms are at the heart of each nursery, extending the importance of food and mealtimes as a cultural and social priority for Italian families and communities. The quality of the surroundings confirms the value of children and develops a sense of self-worth in each child.

There is no 'curriculum' as understood from a British perspective, where a body of knowledge to be imparted to all our children has been decided upon and imposed from 'outside' the world of children or the teachers who know them well. Following her visit to Italy, Shirley Maxwell (1997: 31) commented that:

> there is no requirement to conform to external guidelines or prescriptions. This would be seen as disrespectful of the teacher's professional role. Teachers can keep their attention firmly on the children and their responses. Individual teachers are not held responsible for children's growth and development. The collaborative ethos makes this a shared responsibility.

This is an extremely important observation in the current British context where in a few short years we have moved towards a Foundation Stage for our preschool children with restricted outcomes prescribed by the inspection process and Baseline Assessment.

Children in Reggio Emilia stay in their preschool until they are 6. This is important for children with special needs of any kind. In the UK, many children have entered Reception classes in the past ten years or so at 4 years of age and have then started on a formal curriculum. Many of us working within the early years field think this is too early and our concerns have been well argued and documented. As a result, there are fears that children's needs have not been met and that potential difficulties in learning or socialization may have developed or even been encouraged by placing children in a context that is inappropriate. Within a western model of child development, now supported by recent research into brain development, it is generally accepted that children are still developing physiologically at 4 and need to interact with their environment in order to ensure that connections are formed within the brain as learning occurs. This is especially important when considering language, which develops in a situation where there is dialogue with 'significant others', with the major aspects of structure, or grammar, not in place until 5. Children develop at different rates and have a variety of real-life experiences; there is nothing new in that statement. By restricting their ability to experience and put together their own understanding of the world in discussion with trusted adults who know them well, we run the risk of turning a special need into a special educational need.

Understanding the difference between these two terms – perhaps concepts peculiar to the British – is crucial to developing a philosophy which supports all very young children within a society. Everyone has *special needs* at some time or other during his or her life. A simplistic explanation of this is poor sight, which can be corrected by glasses or contact lenses. A *special educational need* only develops, to my way of thinking, if that primary special need is not met. Most people needing glasses receive them and difficulties in accessing the curriculum do not arise. Some children will develop special educational needs because of a learning difficulty which is inherent or a disability, but this is not necessarily so. Our lack of expectations and inflexibility in altering our narrow system to allow for differing needs can lead to educational failure for a number of children. Children learn very quickly from the attitudes towards them, from both children and adults, that they are not reaching the 'standards' required of the group, and are 'failing'.

Part of the current UK government's intentions, as laid out in the Green Paper (DfEE 1997), involve 'early identification' of difficulties. For many years I have wholeheartedly supported this notion and still do. What the visit to Reggio Emilia, along with other recent experiences, has taught me to do is reflect on the meaning of this and then how we are going to support those 'difficulties' once they have been ascertained.

How 'inclusion' is defined

Over the past few years, the term 'inclusion' has became a subject of debate across Europe and beyond. This is not to say that all European nations yet share a common understanding of what 'inclusion' is, nor do they share a common terminology to begin to create a more uniform approach to supporting children into adulthood. The exact meaning of the term implies meeting all children's needs within the mainstream, so that children are part of their family's natural community and are socialized and educated alongside their peers. This is distinct from 'integration' which carries with it the concept that children are within mainstream physically but are not always given 'access' to all the activities available to the other children in the class. Often, these children are given a 'parallel education', where their schooling becomes more the responsibility of a learning support assistant than their own teacher. The early years, where all children's future potential is not yet set in stone, should offer opportunities for children to take part in as normal an experience as possible. Adults so often restrict young children's access, imposing limits on learning by decisions from their perspective, that mainstream preschool will serve no real purpose. I have in mind a little boy, whom I shall call Sam, whose development was severely hampered by cerebral palsy which not only restricted his movement but also his speech. Sam's parents were brave. With support from a number of professional people whose opinions they valued, they decided to approach Sam's education by paying more regard to his developmental rather than his chronological age. They took account of his personality in deciding that he needed to secure his future as a fully functioning adult. His physical and communication needs were the most pressing and a programme was created outside the state system to support these needs. His Montessori nursery allowed him to stay until he was nearly 6 as this approach suited him well. Sam did not speak until he was 6 but then his speech was complex and correct. He had spent six years watching and waiting until his moment was ripe. He now converses, reads, jokes and shows a markedly mature ability to comment on his acquaintances and the world. All children with any form of need should be offered this flexibility to 'be' but also understood enough to have their horizons expanded. Reggio Emilia has the potential to offer this. Mittler (1995: 105) states that 'one view is that inclusive education starts with radical school reform, changing the existing system and rethinking the entire curriculum of the school in order to meet the needs of all children'.

Within the UK, the Warnock Report in 1978 (DES 1978) and subsequent legislation have brought the concept of a continuum of special need into the public arena. No longer are children to be categorized, and their learning potential delineated by their disability, and placed into a school or unit purely on the grounds of the 'diagnosis' of their condition (the 'medical model'). They now have their individual needs assessed in partnership with parents and educators, rather than relying mainly on the recommendation of the medical profession. Although the system we employ has become highly bureaucratic, lengthy and subject to financial expediency, it has opened up discussions on children's rights, the sort of curriculum that should be available to all, the most effective forms of support for children, and where they should learn. This is an important discussion particularly when opportunities open to children under statutory school age are explored. Current government thinking moves us towards 'inclusion', although without always persuading the teaching profession and parents.

Early identification and assessment of needs, followed by intervention programmes specific to any perceived difficulty, have been seen to
be the way to overcome early problems. We often mislead ourselves and
parents of the very young by offering 'assessment and identification' of
needs at an early age and then implementing an intervention programme
designed to remediate aspects of the child's functioning seen as lacking.
Is this so far away from the old idea of 'diagnosis'? Unfortunately governments, parents and educators do not always share a philosophy regarding intervention and what it should entail, and it is rare if children's
views are heard at this age. The crucial point here is what we should
provide for those children whose development or needs are different from
the majority of children we encounter. Does the Reggio Emilia approach
offer us new insights in this respect?

Special needs in the Reggio Emilia context

For over 30 years Italy has worked towards integrating the majority
of its 'disabled' pupils, aged 6 to 14 years, into mainstream classes. This
accounts for those with a discernible impairment or disability but, as
Vianello and Moniga (1995: 56) explain, it is not always clear how those
with learning difficulties are identified and supported as they are 'considered to come within the province of normality, even if on the border-
line of this'.

I, with others, was particularly interested in how the system incorp-
orates and supports children with special needs and wanted to observe
inclusion, or integration, in practice. I was trying to establish whether
children with special needs were included in the nurseries and how they
were being supported. It was difficult to find answers to all my questions
about inclusion, not only because the visit was so short, but also because
the 'language' is not shared. By this I do *not* refer to translating from
English to Italian, and vice versa, but to the extent to which exact
meanings of the terminology we were using were mutually understood.
Inclusion is an area where much research is needed and despite the
obvious challenge of working within a multilingual European context a
number of projects are now underway.

In Reggio Emilia we did not meet any children who in the UK could
be said to be 'incompatible with the efficient education of the other
children' as established by the Education Act 1981. We saw children with
physical impairments, Down's syndrome and developmental delay. One
little boy who had started school with a much lower level of development
than those of the same age (evidenced by a collection of drawings and
descriptions of his language), confidently approached us to show his
portfolio and explain about his work with pride. Within a short space of

time his drawings had moved from apparently random scribble to recognizable representations of his family and everyday experiences.

It is difficult, having had such a limited time in the preschools, to explore a shared concept of special needs, and I hesitate to suggest that the way children's needs are met in Reggio appears to owe more to the medical authorities responsible for identifying their needs than to judgements made by their educators. I wondered, 'Who makes decisions about which school, or group of schools, are approached to admit children with special needs?' Staff told us that once alerted to the admission of a child with special needs, an extra member of staff is allocated to the preschool in order to support that child.

My impression of Reggio Emilia's response to children with special needs is that the preschools minimize many of the effects of disability and a slower rate of learning because the learning environment matches the developmental and social needs of the individual child. A number of reflections lead me to consider that perhaps the ethos and practice also limits the development of challenging behaviour. A difference between the systems in the UK and the Reggio response is the commitment to children learning as a group, from each other. The language used by the children was rich (even allowing for our limited knowledge of Italian), both in the complexity of the structures they used to explain what they were doing and what they understood, but also in exploring difficult concepts, such as war and death (subjects often neatly evaded with young children in much of the UK). The children listened to each other, made suggestions about particular problems encountered in their work, and asked for advice. Adults were there to suggest and support but not to take away from children the responsibility for solving problems. Emphases on good language skills, particularly a functional use of language, problem solving within a real context and working as a full member of a peer group are areas which are difficult for some children with special needs, and so these are often avoided, not only by the children but also by staff who prepare an environment which sidesteps these kinds of learning challenge.

Reggio Emilia is a stable, prosperous and cohesive community. The preschools are a highly regarded part of that community, which in turn values the group experience they offer to young children. Provision is local; so the children are not placed in distant centres which isolate them and their families from their own community. Provision can be full-time, avoiding a situation common in the UK where very young children with special needs often attend more than one, and sometimes several, different forms of provision during a week. Penn (1997: 109), contrasting the Italian provision with some daycare provision in the UK, described much UK provision as 'a social work resource for particularly vulnerable families, which stressed care, surveillance and family harmony. The nurseries were not seen primarily as a place where children learn'.

The central role of parents in their children's education is well established in Reggio Emilia. The successful inclusion of any child with a special need is achieved if parents and staff are both secure and enthusiastic about what is offered and committed to working together to make it happen. Parents, both mothers and fathers, as well as members of the extended family, appeared at ease with staff and shared discussions and decision making. There were numerous examples during our visit of children being far more central to the lives of adults than in the UK. Parents and children walked together in the squares in the evening, children were free to climb and explore the ancient statues, they ate with their parents in restaurants and talked to adults in the park. If children are to be included, then this is as it should be – into communities and not just into schools.

The stability and certainty of the community are mirrored in the commitment of the staff to their schools. Their approach has firm foundations and its international recognition has endorsed the practice and given rise to this confidence. Staff tend to stay a long time, providing stability and ensuring their place in the community. New staff are inducted carefully into the accepted ways of working, though this may have to change in the future with alterations to teacher training in Italy and aims for an all-graduate profession. The commitment to ongoing research within the schools and its application to teaching is refreshing, coming from a background where governments and professionals can pay scant regard to educational research, and are sometimes scathing and dismissive of it. The deep knowledge that staff develop about each child, about the way individuals learn and where each child is in her or his thinking, benefits all children. This knowledge leads to a freedom for children within the nursery setting, as staff are not anxious about having all children in view all of the time. Children are trusted to take care of themselves and it is recognized that they need time away from adult eyes. It is also accepted that children will sometimes spend hours engrossed in one activity. Two little girls spent three hours or so (the whole of one of our visits) playing together with a collection of red and pink glass objects displayed on a light box. No attempt was made to intervene and move them on to something else. Conversely, it was accepted that children sometimes need to 'flit' and activities were established to enable them to do this. One was a weaving loom, with a basket of various threads next to it so that children could add just one row or perhaps more in passing. Through this sensitivity to their needs, children develop a confidence in adults but also a confidence in themselves. Vlachou's research into inclusion in the UK contrasts with this approach. She writes of the 'mechanization of the teaching act, which reinforced a restrictive notion of learning, a specific image of children and a linear process of development' (1997: 167). Although government policy talks about 'entitlement' to a broad and balanced curriculum, teachers talk about stronger external pressures to 'fit children in a specific system'.

Conclusion

In conclusion, I share Corbett's (1998: 6) view that:

> Special educational needs are not just about what happens in our classrooms, about procedures, practices and assessments. They are about our cultures, the societies we create and the relationships we form between people, countries, systems, hierarchies and global economies; about our ways of being in the world.

Reggio Emilia is seductive. On visiting the preschools, I was impressed by the richness of their interiors and their surroundings, and this was quickly followed by awe at the freedom of the educators to implement an approach in which they truly believe. I moved away from being sceptical about these children's achievements to recognizing how far we can underestimate what young children can do. The question remains – what have I learned and how can the central tenets of this approach be transferred and used to support all children including those on the margins? Reggio educators are right to say that it is difficult to transplant their system wholesale elsewhere. Their situation is born from social and political strengths which are not necessarily found in the UK, even on a regional basis. There are many areas here, both reasonably prosperous and disadvantaged, where families and teachers move frequently. Many, particularly city areas, do not have a stable population where heritage, culture and values are shared. Many of the schools I work with in London are now staffed by teachers who come from all over the world with different experiences, expectations and priorities. This situation contrasts with many of the strong features of Reggio Emilia, but could be viewed positively as having strengths if only we took the time to consider carefully the needs of all the very young children now within our boundaries. There are, I believe, universal elements which can and should be re-established in the UK context – learning once again to trust and value children and their educators is an essential starting point.

References

Corbett, J. (1998) *Special Educational Needs in the Twentieth Century*. London: Cassell.
DES (Department of Education and Science) (1978) *Special Educational Needs* (The Warnock Report). London: HMSO.

DfE (Department for Education) (1994) *Code of Practice on the Identification and Assessment of Special Educational Needs*. London: DfE.

DfEE (Department for Education and Employment) (1997) *Excellence for all Children: Meeting Special Educational Needs*. London: HMSO.

Maxwell, S. (1997) Preparation for teaching, in P. Gura (ed.) (1997) *Reflections on Early Education and Care*. London: BAECE.

Mittler, P. (1995) Special needs education: an international perspective, *British Journal of Special Education*, 22(3): 105–8.

Penn, H. (1997) *Comparing Nurseries: Staff and Children in Italy, Spain and the UK*. London: Paul Chapman Publishing.

Reggio Children (1995) *A Journey into the Rights of Children*. Reggio Emilia: Reggio Children.

Vlachou, A.D. (1997) *Struggles for Inclusive Education*. Buckingham: Open University Press.

Vianello, I. and Moniga, P. (1995) Special education in Italy: integration of people with disabilities and the education of teachers, in P. Mittler and P. Daunt (eds) (1995) *Teacher Education for Special Needs in Europe*. London: Paul Chapman Publishing.

9 Creating places for living and learning

John Bishop

It is possible to design spaces alternatively from the traditional ways: spaces that are softer, less rigid, more open to indertminableness of experience. The environment is conceived not as a monologic space structured according to a formal framework and a functional order, but as a place where multiple dimensions coexist – even opposing ones. A hybrid environment in which space is given shape and identity by the relationships created within it. A space, then, that is constructed not by selecting and simplifying the elements, but through a fusion of distinct poles (inside and outside, formality and flexibility, material and immaterial) which creates rich and complex conditions.

(Ceppi and Zini 1998: 2)

These words appear in the publication *Children, Spaces and Relations*, which describes the 'meeting of minds' in Reggio Emilia between the pedagogical, philosophical and architectural.

There is much we can learn from the environment of the preschool buildings of Reggio Emilia which can be used to illustrate the potential that exists between people and the buildings they use. The philosophy underlying the Reggio approach to preschool education and the creation of places for such learning is what we should concentrate on understanding; the holistic needs of people rather than a set of standards. Both the thinking and creative outcomes of this approach are rooted in an educational and design philosophy that we can absorb and utilize but which we cannot 'package' and transplant.

The preschool buildings of Reggio Emilia occupy the 'middle ground' of architecture without being compromise solutions. As such they are 'living' buildings with authenticity and meaning in contrast to a culture where architecture is increasingly perceived in terms of finite aesthetic 'images' and 'objects' empty of content. The buildings illustrate clearly this alternative approach to a sustainable architecture, an approach that requires the architect to empathize with the creativity of the building user and which empowers the user to inform the design process. The layers of meaning that build up 'the life' of our built environment must be envisaged as being infinitely more complex both personally and communally than any theoretical typology can suggest – the concept of a 'completed building' as such does not exist in the Reggio vocabulary.

It would be undesirable to write a conventional design brief for a building to house a Reggio preschool because the production of such a brief would be limited to lists of accommodation and standards of provision. Such briefing information, technical data and safety standards exist for all Reggio schools but the designers of these buildings do not consider those as a starting point for the creation of an environment in which young children will live and learn.

The fabric of the Reggio preschool buildings share a common simplicity of structural form which communicates, to all who use them, an 'economy of means' based on the values and ethics of the educational approach they house. The materials of the buildings and the ways in which they are put together are evidence of a desire for the integration of poetics and technology. The unique qualities of each building come not from the formal arrangement of parts but from the pragmatic relationship between person and place, detail and material, building and building, and building and site. These are buildings located in their urban or rural context and culture in the tradition of the kindergarten movement; buildings that do not look back to a romantic past but embrace tradition alongside the present in anticipation of the future; centres of evolving community development that utilize both tradition and innovation to assist children, parents and teachers to bridge between the macro-environment of the city and micro-environment of the home.

Figure 9.1 shows the location of the Diana School in the Giarddini Pubblici. The choice of the site was a community decision to place the school in this park close to the children's city-centre homes; the name of the school is that of a cinema that stood on the site before. The school has the external appearance of a utility park building. The design and detail of the playground, school fence and gate all 'fit in' to the Italian urban context and provide a seamless transition with the life of the surrounding city.

The intention has always been that the internal and external spaces of Reggio preschools should have educational significance and symbolic meaning for those who use them. Spaces contained within the framework of the building are visualized as a changing pattern of overlapping places in which the children learn in what is a microcosm of their street, square or

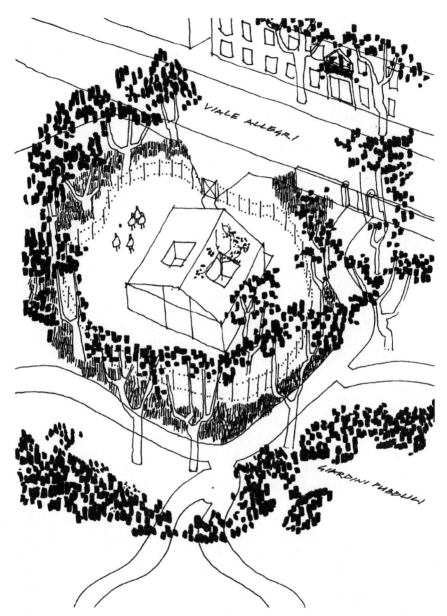

Figure 9.1   Location of the Diana School in the Giarddini Pubblici

town. Such places are not 'frozen' in adult design solutions to a perceived and stereotypical educational need – a playhouse or a climbing frame – they are perceived by the designer as areas of the building and garden that the child or children can appropriate. Such appropriation is part of the

Figure 9.2   Interior of the Diana School

child's socialization and growth of independence and is evidence of the need in us all to 'make places'; a need that in later life is the motivation that underpins our role in the evolving built environment in which we live.

Figure 9.2 illustrates the interior of the Diana School looking across the *piazza,* which is the central communal space of the building. The use of a structural frame with infilling wall panels rather than load-bearing walls provides a permeable enclosure between external and internal spaces. The roof has a shallow slope and this is exposed to view on the inside which means that some areas have low ceilings while other areas are higher. The concrete columns and beams are left exposed which, combined with the other building materials, gives a range of surfaces from rough to smooth. The 'architecture' of the building does not intrude into the day-to-day life of the school and is there to provide shelter for and to assist with the process of creative learning. The evolving patterns of places within and around the building are in harmony with those of the city of which they are so much a part.

The analogy with the urban context is illustrated by the following statement by Loris Malaguzzi, where he refers to the central space of the school (the *piazza*) shared by children, parents and teachers as the community of the school. As with the urban model on which it is based, the *piazza* is a place of pathways and events that change with the time of day, day of the week and season of the year. It contains interventions and objects of meaning that relate visually to its scale and reinforce the sense of communality in the school.

> To learn and relearn together with the children is our line of work. We proceed in such a way that the children are not shaped by experience but are the ones to give shape to it . . . Our way of working makes possible the choice among different modes of interaction. Small groups of children work simultaneously and can be found all around the school setting, organised so as to facilitate social, cognitive, verbal and symbolic constructions. Our children in fact have many choices: they have places where they can be alone, in a small number, in a large group with the teachers or without them in the *atelier*, in the mini *atelier*, in the large *piazza* or, if the weather is good, in the outside courtyard, rich with small and large play structures . . . We live in the tradition of the city, with its squares and porticoes, which provide an irreplaceable model for meetings, negotiations and dialogues of various human encounters; moreover, the central square of our city transforms itself twice a week into the hundred stalls of the market.
>
> (Edwards *et al.* 1993: 86)

In the above quotation Malaguzzi refers to the *atelier* (the studio, workshop or art room), which is seen as the philosophical hub of the school and is located, as with important buildings in towns and cities, adjacent to the *piazza*. This space is part artist studio, part artisan workshop and part science laboratory and it is here that teachers and children work together in constructing 'visual languages' to explore and communicate ideas and meanings. This exploration is led by the *atelierista* who is a creative artist with an educational training and whose role is to extend the work of the *atelier* throughout the school community:

> The work in the *atelier* is seen as integrated and combined with the entire didactic approach. The intent was to react to the marginal place assigned generally to visual and expressive education . . . The *atelier* is an additional space within the school where to explore with our hands and our minds, where to refine our sight through the practice of the visual arts, where to work on projects connected with activities planned in the classroom, where to explore and combine new and well known tools, techniques and materials.
>
> (Edwards *et al.* 1993: 74)

The normal practice in the design of modern school buildings has been to separate off service spaces, of which the kitchen is the most important, from the teaching spaces. Although this is done for safety reasons it also reflects the accepted view as to the subservient nature of these parts of the building and the people who work there. This is not the case in the Reggio preschools where the cooks, cleaners and care-takers are seen as integral members of the teaching staff, with their role being observed by the children as the work takes place during school hours. The kitchen is located so that the preparation and cooking of food is observed by the children and the smell of cooking can permeate the building. The role of cooking is seen as bringing authenticity to the life of the school and the kitchen as a place of warmth and domestic security.

As with every other part of the building, the entrance is seen as more than fulfilling the functional requirement of entry and exit because it is envisaged as a place of meeting, communication and observation. It is a place of threshold, as is the school gate, on the path to and from school. A stage on the sensory transition from outside to inside through a land-scape of places created to extend the learning experience; places defined and enclosed by plants and materials of varying form and texture. The symbolic meaning of the garden – a place of nature in the child's world – is still central to the concept of kindergarten contained in the Reggio approach.

In both design and use no space in the buildings is considered peri-pheral and every part of the school environment is a place with potential for living and learning. Evidence of the educational process in the form of diagrams, working models, paintings, etc. – learning works as opposed to art works – form visual interventions within the structure and enclos-ure of the learning spaces. There are very few notice-boards, as such, in a Reggio preschool because every place defined by wall, floor and ceiling and the surfaces themselves are a potential place to record where the child/teacher exploration has been and to stimulate new routes it could take. The activities of the day take place in a suspension of creative documentation – work in progress, work in abeyance, work to be com-pleted – this is not a 'shop window' but an 'aquarium', and there is an open invitation to join the fish and swim!

For the above reasons the Reggio preschool buildings are not institu-tional 'backdrops' but interactive environments in which pupils and teachers work together to develop an understanding of what it means to be in a place – to experience being part of a culture located in time and space, in contrast to the pervasive environment of 'non-place' which is what most of our expanding global culture has become. In contrast to this, the Reggio preschool environment is one of 'living patterns' as defined by Christopher Alexander in his book *A Timeless Way of Building*:

The more living patterns there are in a thing – a room, a building, or a town – the more it comes to life as an entirety, the more it glows, the more it has that self-maintaining fire, which is the quality without a name . . . These patterns of events are always interlocked with certain geometric patterns in the space. Indeed as we shall see, each building and each town is ultimately made out of these patterns in space and out of nothing else: they are the atoms and molecules from which a building or a town is made.

(Alexander 1979: 10)

Such a contextual approach to learning is extended into the urban locality of the school when children and teachers take walks together through the city and find answers to questions like: What is the city like in the rain? Why is the city so much quieter when it has snowed? What happens below the grids in the pavement? In such experiential learning the route followed through streets and squares becomes an extension of the path through the *atelier* and the *piazza* back in school – this is not a journey to a preordained cultural destination; it is a journey that expands the culture of the child.

Finally, to visit a Reggio preschool is to realize that sensory awareness and the experience of space are fundamental to the educational approach, because there are no 'no-go' areas in and around these buildings – if the body cannot get there then the eyes and ears can. These are not open-plan schools as such, and yet there are very few enclosed places due to spaces being defined with surfaces of varying transparency, reflectance, colour and texture. Such space division was not frozen when the building was designed but is still evolving as part of the life of the building with sheets of plastic, bead curtains, wire netting and any other material that children and teachers can find to extend the range of transparency from clear to opaque, or the acoustic quality from sharp to flat. Such sensory awareness is fundamental to making places, by designers and users alike, and in more general terms generates a built environment of sensory experiences based on an awareness of scale, colour, texture, sound, smell, light, micro-climate and so on.

But, more important still I believe, the Reggio approach illustrates the philosophy that people make places through habitation and partnership rather than by delegating 'total' design to the creativity of others. Human existence has the potential to be an intrinsically imaginative project *for all involved*, and education can release that potential. It is through creating such living places that people bring with them their ideas and their artefacts to create a temporal, climatic and topographic location in which 'work and play, reality and fantasy, science and imagination, sky and earth, reason and dreams are things that do belong together' Edwards *et al.* (1993: 3).

References

Alexander, C. (1979) *A Timeless Way of Building.* Oxford: Oxford University Press.

Ceppi, C. and Zini, M. (1998) *Children, Spaces and Relations: A Meta project for an Environment for Young Children.* Reggio Emilia: Reggio Children Modena Domus Academy Research Centre.

Edwards, C., Gandini, L. and Forman, G. (eds) (1993) *The Hundred Languages of Children: The Reggio Emilia Approach to Early Childhood Education.* Norwood, NJ: Ablex.

'She's back!' The impact of
my visit to Reggio Emilia on
a group of 3- and 4-year-olds

 Christine Parker

> This is not about convincing, it is about an invitation to visit.
> (Rinaldi 1999)

This chapter is a description of my experience with a group of 3- and
4-year-old nursery school children before and after my visit to Reggio
Emilia in April 1999. I was excited by the unique opportunity of exploring the notion of my forthcoming absence with the children. My theory
was that they would be interested, would want to know where and
when I was going and be curious on my return about my experiences.

For the purposes of this study I am using Rinaldi's (1999) definition of
a theory: 'A system of concepts, strategies, actions that provides a satis-
factory explanation for the person who is doing the thinking'.

'Are you going to Italy?'

My focus group were the full-time children in my class: 16 3- and
4-year-olds. I told them that I would be travelling to Italy and showed
them where Italy is on the globe in relation to England and Pakistan.
The children in our school are familiar with the concept of distant travel
as many have either visited Pakistan or have family members whose
visits are within recent memory. At school the children frequently
initiate role-play that originates from their knowledge of airports and
aeroplanes. They talk about their personal experiences; directing each
other, describing, imagining and recalling. For example, Mahmood constructed a rocket using materials from the technology area and informed
an adult: 'A rocket on the aeroplane going to Pakistan. My dad and
Mrs Salman going to Pakistan and my mum and me. All them going.'

Mahmood has a theory about how we can travel to Pakistan and who ought to accompany him.

The children were shown my travel bag and the items that I intended taking to Italy, including clothes, toilet bag, notebooks, pen and pencil, reading book, Italian dictionary and phrase book. The bag was made available in the home area for the children to pack and carry around the school.

The children were told that people who live in Italy speak Italian. The children could identify with this concept as we frequently talk about different languages and the children themselves are bilingual. I asked the children what words would be useful for me to know in Italian. They suggested 'toilet' – *'gabinetto'*. We practised *'Dove gabinetto?'* – 'Where is the toilet?' The children had a collective theory that everyone needs the toilet. Asad insisted that I would need socks. I asked, 'How many pairs would I need for eight days?' I was told two but I would need to know the Italian for 'wash' because I would need to wash my socks. Again the children were formulating their own theories about my requirements while away. The children were becoming familiar with the idea that I was going to Italy and if I was seen with my coat on they would ask, 'Are you going to Italy?'

'She's back!'

On my return the children responded in various ways. They explored my travel bag, which included some extras: children's books, tickets, luggage labels, postcards, and coffee cups. Aneesa told Mrs Turner about the luggage label she was given: 'Mrs Parker gave it to me. It says my name.' When asked where she was going she replied, 'To Leeds town on the train.' She was asked, 'Where did Mrs Parker go?' She answered, 'To Italy.' The postcards I had sent gradually arrived and Salim was particularly interested in these, having told his mother all about them. Many of the children were involved in modelling aeroplanes and airports in the small construction area and the technology area. The children enjoyed the story about me in Italy which was presented in a book of photographs. With Mrs Salman the group thought about questions they wanted to ask me, such as, 'Did you enjoy the food on the aeroplane? Did they give you a toothbrush? Did you sleep on the aeroplane? Did you have orange juice to drink?' The questions reflected the children's experiences of long-haul flights.

The children were ready to ask their own questions. In this observation Shohaib returns to the same question, perhaps unsatisfied with my answers or needing confirmation. Shohaib asked, 'Mrs Parker why you go Italy? I like Italy. I like all the children. My mummy don't take me Italy.'

Figure 10.1   Asad's map

Shohaib's mother informed me that Shohaib talked about my visit at home and again expressed his intention to travel to Italy. Twelve days later Shohaib was a dentist in the role-play area examining my teeth and he said, 'I want to look in your mouth. What's your name? Why you go Italy? Why you see lovely schools? All the children in Italy? Two? It got all of them? One, two, three, four, five, six, seven, eight, nine.' Shohaib wanted to construct a theory that would explain my absence. He was testing his theory. Scott (1996: 36) reiterates a concern for adults to ask relevant and thought-provoking questions. In these exchanges I was rediscovering the power of the questions asked by children.

Asad drew a map and said, 'This is my map. The house becomes a rocket. This is the rocket and I'm going to the rocket. Flew to Mrs Parker in Italy. I pressed the button it went faster and faster, the fire came.' Asad is expressing his theories. He has a notion of what a map is and its purpose. He has a theory that objects can transform – that is, the house became a rocket. He has an understanding of cause and effect (see Figure 10.1).

From experiences such as these I considered the strategy of 'reproposing' that was so much to the fore in the Reggio schools, where children are encouraged to consider dialogue from a previous day's discourse, and decided to initiate this strategy myself. Irfan had constructed a Lego aeroplane and informed me, 'Look up here Mrs Parker, people go in the back. The monster fighting. I made that for you.' Irfan expressed his theory about how aeroplanes are boarded, introduced an element of fantasy and explored how to form a relationship with another person. The following day Irfan brought the model to me and I reproposed his dialogue from the previous day, quoting word for word. He followed on by saying, 'They climb up here and sit up and fly like this.' Irfan's immediate response was to extend his theory about how people board aeroplanes. This utterance was also significant because Irfan is acquiring English as an additional language and has had difficulties communicating his ideas to both monolingual and bilingual adults, often using his own 'cartoon language' that he shared with his cousin. This was a leap in his confidence and learning.

I was reproposing children's talk and decided to revisit their mark-making. Ahmad worked in the mark-making area and as he drew he described his actions and his work. 'Do this then put your crocoly finger. Then it's raining, look we washing Mrs Matthew's car. I've got new thing in my house, computer.' Ahmad made marks that represented writing and he read his writing out aloud. 'About the rain and the crocolyn. I can make it on there. Let me write it first, writing about a car. Have you done it? I'm writing. What's the dinner time today? Look at what I made. I made a foot, Mrs Parker's.' Ahmad wrote and read, 'Mrs Parker's foot. Give me another piece of paper. Now I'm making Mrs Matthew's car. Look I made it. I'm drawing a football man, kick, kick! A football mans. Look I made all the mans. This is football and this is all the mans that play football. I made a daddy bear and a mummy bear. This is mummy bear, daddy bear and baby. The bear's house, porridge, chocolate and sweets, buns, chocolates. They live together.'

Nine days later Ahmad was presented with a photocopy of his mark-making. Ahmad said, 'I want to write this.' Ahmad's dialogue from the previous occasion was read out to him. He said, 'All that different, same, same colour. Now I'm going to draw a rainbow. This is how rainbow I make. I'm going to make another one bear's house. This is mummy bear.' He read his writing, 'The bear's adventure and this is called when Goldilocks went to the house of the bears.' Ahmad moved onto another point of interest, 'I've got boots on today. What have you got on?' Then returned to the bears, which he redrew on the reverse side of his paper. 'Bear's birthday, let's sing happy birthday to the bear.' Ahmad pointed to the felt pens and said, 'All the candles blows up.'

Ahmad relates his representations to his real-life experiences. He has a theory about writing and knows he can combine writing and drawing. He recalls past events – for example, 'we washing Mrs Matthew's car' and reveals a concept of time and an interest in routine. Ahmad experiments with book and song language and words he has heard. What is a crocolyn? A crocodile? A chiropodist? He has the confidence to play with words.

In this observation Ahmad is constantly making associations that are meaningful to him; he seeks adult approval and support and he knows he can make requests. He has a theory about things being the same and different. He is able to accommodate several lines of thought passing from one theory to another with apparent ease. Concerns that are immediate are intertwined with storying. This example has an additional significance because on entry he spoke little English, in single words. The complexity of his talk a year later is an indication of his great achievement in English acquisition. In the second observation Ahmad has the confidence to develop his talk about the bears, further using language learned from stories and songs. He also has the confidence to ask questions, such as, 'What's the dinnertime today?', 'Have you done it?', 'What have you got on?'

My attention was drawn to children working alongside each other. Aneesa and Zahra worked alongside each other making marks on large sheets of paper. This is their conversation:

Aneesa: She copied me.
Zahra: Roundabout, I went to roundabouts with my dad and my mum and my brother. Look I've done spots. I'm making a boat now.
Aneesa: So am I.
Zahra: Why are you copying like me?
Aneesa: Little ones. Little tiny ones. My tiny little boat with a chicken on the top.
Zahra: Chicken on the top! I'm making a bouncy castle, bouncing castle. Big bouncing castle. I'm making cherries on the top. I'm making in the middle octopus. Look octopus. Roundabouts with cherries on the top.
Aneesa: I'm making a spider now. I'm making an octopus. It's not sunny, it's windy.

It is possible to identify a shared theory in both their talk and mark-making. Aneesa and Zahra have a theory about playing with language they are familiar with. They combine words from a song with confidence and are able to share their ideas with confidence. It is significant that Aneesa is Punjabi-speaking and Zahra is Gujerati-speaking and that English is their shared language.

At this stage I had focused on individual children's talk and mark-making. In the Reggio schools the emphasis is on children working in a group. So it was to group work that I now turned.

In the Reggio Emilia schools we observed overhead projectors and slide projectors, screens and light used as an integral part of the basic provision. At our school we decided to use the projectors in one small area that can be blacked out. We experimented with projecting light, slides and objects in conjunction with exploring the theme of a magic carpet which we had experienced at the local art gallery exhibition, 'In the Picture'.

The following observation was made as slides of Pakistan were being projected onto the wall. Imagine a small dark room that has a 'magic carpet' and floor cushions. Two walls are covered with a white sheet for a screen. Children have free access to this area, coming and going as they please. The adult, me, sits in one corner writing and operating the slide projector. The children observe the changing images and talk about what they see. Simultaneously they are involved in role-play and are socializing. They are fascinated by the mechanism of the slide projector.

The magic carpet to Pakistan

[*Slide of a giant turtle on the beach, Karachi, Pakistan.*]

Dawud: Do it! What's it? That magic. Tortoise. It lives far away. Look at that.

Asad: I'm not sitting on the magic carpet. I'm just watching.

Zahid: Look lights, what's this?

Zahra: Let's go to sleep.

Maggie: Where's it gone? Come on let's go to sleep.

Zahra: It's changing here. I'm going to sleep now.

Irfan: Me and my brother got small torch. Press the button.

Irfan looked at the projector closely.

Irfan: Only light.

Asad: What's happening?

Zahid: We don't recognize.

Zahra: Come on let's go to . . .

Everyone flopped onto the cushions. Zahra noticed that the images were projected onto the other children. Zahid commented on his shadow. Waqas looked into the light.

Ahmad: Dust.

Ahmad waved his hands in front of the light.

Zahid: Look it change over. How it change over?

Ahmad: What is this?

Irfan ran towards the screen.

Asad: Let's go to sleep now everybody.

Zahra: Why is steam going in there?

Maggie: Everybody up now!

Ahmad spread his arms out wide over the picture.

Maggie: Now change the picture over.
Zahra: Look them cards [*slides*]. If I do that make it come light on it.

She waved her fingers in front of the screen.

Irfan: You two!

[*Slide of Fairy Meadows, a mountainous region of Northern Pakistan.*]
Zahid: I don't know where we are.
Asad: At the grass.

Zahra initiated the singing of 'The Bear Went Over the Mountain'.

Maggie: A light.
Zahid: Come on!
Zahra: Let's sing it again.
Waqas: The bear went over the mountain.

Irfan left the group for a few minutes to find paper and a pencil.

[*Slide of a market scene.*]
Irfan: You been there? You inside? You do cheese? You do smile?
Karim: I've got big Playstation. My dad bring this.
Waqas: Look at this.
Irfan: Watch my finger, my finger do.

Karim walked towards the screen.

Karim: Like a photograph.

[*Slide of a hookah* [tobacco] *shop.*]
Irfan: Are you there? On the top? Where are you Mrs Parker?

[*Slide of a man making a* charpoi (*a rope bed*).]
Karim: Mr Parker?
Irfan: No, a man.
Karim: Your brother, Mr Parker.

[*Slide of Babu nut stall.*]
Waqas: This your shop?
Irfan: A light on with a sofa on the top.

[*Slide of people playing cricket.*]
Asad: It changed . . . cricket.

[*Slide of Quaid-Azam-Mazar, Jinnah's Tomb.*]
Aishah: That mosque.

The following theories can be identified about how images are made, tortoises and their habitats, how to form relationships, daily routines, change, different places. If there are mountains there must be bears, smile and say 'cheese' you have to when you have your photograph taken, if Mrs Parker shows us a picture she must be there somewhere and if there is a man there it must be Mr Parker! On the following day the same slides were shown and we revisited the scenes.

Zahra: Me and Aneesa are going to Canada, you have to wait. [*Sings*] Flying, flying. Be quiet we're going now. We're going to Canada.

[*Slide of Badshahi Masjid, a Moghul mosque in Lahore, Pakistan.*]
Irene: I've been there with my mummy and daddy. I had some toys there, in Ilkley.
Aminah: [*To the projector*] Go away.

[*Slide of Islamabad, the capital of Pakistan.*]
Irene: I've been there, that's the seaside.
Rahim: I've been to Karachi.
Zahra: I've been to Meadowhall with my mummy and my brother. We were jumping there.

[*Slide of Shah Faisal Masjid, a modern mosque in Islamabad.*]
Aneesa: I've been there. It's warm there.
Zahra: When I'm warm I wear a tee-shirt.

[*Slide of Swat, a rural area of Northern Pakistan.*]
Zahra: Climbing.
Rahim: It's got rocks.
Aneesa: It's got stones.
Zahra: We went to Blackpool and then I was tired in the car.
Hassan: Swat.
Zahra: We go to the White Rose Centre as well.
Rahim: Let's sing to that!

These observations illustrate how creative the children are, how they think, do, move, play, exchange ideas, talk, socialize, sing and improvize. Further theories can be identified about places in the world, aspects of travel, having a sense of adventure, making connections with personal experiences, that you can make objects disappear, weather and what you wear, the nature of mountains, travel and getting tired, and being friends. I was impressed by the children's independence – my role was as an observer. The children referred to my presence but they were not dependent on it. Tizard and Hughes (1984) concluded that children are less likely to talk freely in a nursery setting in contrast to the home setting where adults talk to children in a more realistic and meaningful way. My delight in these observations is the children's ability to converse with each other spontaneously and bounce ideas off each other. They asked many questions: 'What's it?'; 'Where's it gone?'; 'What's happening?';

'Why is steam going in there?'; 'You been there?'; 'Are you there?'; 'On the top?'; 'Where are you Mrs Parker?'. These last questions could have been reproposed by working through the photographic process. The opportunity for the children to take their own photographs and discuss who was there at that time at that location could have been provided. In not following up these events at the time I lost the opportunity to repropose the children's theories.

At our school the adults worked in teams of three; the three classrooms are open-plan and present the children with alternative areas of provision. Consequently the teams move rooms on a three-weekly rota enabling all the adults to work in all areas of provision. After the second observation it was our turn to move to another room and I was unable to follow up my theories with the same group of children in the same space. However, the possibilities for using the projector were developed further by other members of staff.

I decided to continue by focusing on the children's talk and mark-making. It is possible to both repropose speech and revisit children's representations. I was searching for the children's theories, the connections between them. I considered how these theories could be extended. In one respect I did build on the experience of the 'magic carpet to Pakistan' because I developed the group work. What was lost was the opportunity to challenge and extend the children's specific theories.

Ogden Water nature reserve

A group of 12 children were taken by minibus to Ogden Water, a small reservoir and nature reserve where we all spent the day together. The children drew representations of their experiences and talked about them. The children revisited their work after it had been photocopied and an adult read out their previous dialogue. The children were able to add more detail to their representations and adapted each other's ideas – for example, by filling in the enclosures to represent the water, and by adding people (see Figures 10.2 and 10.3).

The children's ideas were extended further when they were encouraged to work on the same piece of paper in groups of three. Initially my colleagues and I had anticipated that the children would find this difficult, but the opposite was true. When presented with the option of either working alone or in a group, their preference was for group work. The children gained in confidence from each other and were happy to share ideas and resources. It was noticeable that this group of children were beginning to work together cooperatively.

To aid recall the children referred to photographs of our visit as they wrote and drew.

Figure 10.2 'We see racing car and some ducks and the minibus. The water came out we saw bubbles. We keep walking looking for animals. I saw a duck it was in a stone. A parrot bird he was rock inside.'

Irfan: Me! Look at me! Look at my trainers.

Zahra: Zahid and Irfan! Look at that! Slug. Tractor. Bird was flying. Aneesa. Flowers.

Asad: Look at me! Mrs Parker I'm going to get the bread over there but I can't reach.

Irfan: I'm going here again myself. Let's take all these children.

Zahra: Minibus.

Irfan: Ducks.

Asad: Flowers.

Irfan: Look at this duck, little duck. Look a baby duck. A car, a car.

Zahra: This is his wheel. Shall I show you how do a duck? Shall I draw a table?

Irfan: All sitting down.

Asad: Shall I write Ogden Water? Look, I'm writing Ogden Water. This is Zahra. [*To Zahra*] I've made you some legs.

Figure 10.3 'I had some dinner, juice, bread, cucumber and samosa. I see pond with ducks. We throw some bread to the ducks. Ogden Water we went, we keep walking we saw some bubbles coming out. We went to the minibus and went to Maninnigham Park.'

Zahra: Shall I draw Shohaib? I did Shohaib, look!
Asad: Does this say Ogden Water?
Zahra: I did the Ogden.
Asad: This is the water.
Zahra: This is the Ogden Water,
Asad: I'm making the bread.

Zahra and Asad spelled out 'Went to Og-den Wa-ter.'

Irfan: I'm writing my name.

What captured the children's interest the most? What were the recurring themes and theories? They were the people who went, the ducks, the expanse of water, the minibus and map-like representations. How could these theories have been extended further? More time for talking in depth about our shared experiences and for reflection would have been beneficial. Further visits to explore specific ideas (for example, water, ducks and maps) would have been reminiscent of methods used by Isaacs at the Malting House School in the 1930s, when adults responded to the children's questions, such as 'What is wood made of?' by going out of school to help develop the children's understanding of their world (Tizard and Hughes 1984: 262). What we *did* achieve was the development of a group identity.

This experience leads me to further questions about our methods of working – similar questions to those identified by Tizard and Hughes (1984) concerning how we group children, our open-plan classrooms and how in some workplaces workers do not have a permanent home base. I found myself wanting my own space to develop children's theories over an extended period of time.

Concluding thoughts

Working through some of the ideas I brought back from Reggio leads me to suggest that:

- Reproposing children's talk enables children to expand on their theories and extend them. This process shows children that their ideas and thoughts are valued and can be shared and discussed. It reinforces their previous learning and develops them further. The children were confident in their use of new vocabulary and of tenses, and made connections.
- Revisiting children's mark-making results in similar outcomes. They can add to their work, review and alter theories. Their self-esteem develops and the adult has a starting point to develop the children's representational and cognitive skills. The added detail is significant.
- The processes of reproposing and revisiting children's theories has an impact on developing children's confidence in speaking English as an additional language.
- Working in a group together enables children to appreciate each other's achievements, learn from each other and develop their confidence.
- The value of focusing our attention on the children's concerns and interests is reinforced, allowing opportunities for spontaneous talk between children about those ideas and experiences that fascinate and inspire them.
- To enable practitioners to value children's theories through revisiting and reproposing requires some thought in practical terms of space, time, resources and staffing. All these issues have been considered in the Reggio Emilia settings and opportunities for extended study of a theory are provided for.
- When recognizing the quality of children's learning in the Reggio Emilia schools it is also important for practitioners in the UK to acknowledge their own traditions, achievements and extensive documentation in the field of children's learning.

References

Rinaldi, C. (1999) The pedagogy of listening. Lecture given at the UK Study Tour, Reggio Emilia, April 1999.

Scott, W. (1996) Choices in learning, in C. Nutbrown (ed.) *Respectful Educators, Capable Learners, Children's Rights and Early Education*. London: Paul Chapman Publishing.

Tizard, B. and Hughes, M. (1984) *Young Children Learning*. London: Fontana.

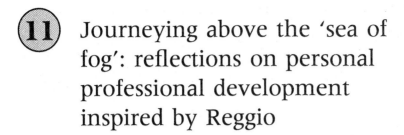

11 Journeying above the 'sea of fog': reflections on personal professional development inspired by Reggio

Robin Duckett

This chapter is journalistic, i.e. an offering of snapshots and episodes, with the intent of sharing an account of stepping-stones – i.e. significant markers in the development of *my* practice and that of colleagues. It is simply a story of an individual nursery teacher looking for good ways to do things!

I, along with many others, have experienced a vital injection of encouragement and inspiration from our encounter with the experience of Reggio Emilia. At the same time, I realize that the 'inspiration of Reggio' is actually our own inspiration, vibrantly reflected – ideas and professionalism, thought, feelings and intellect from the same bedrock, but nurtured more vigorously, generously and comprehensively within a sister culture. This chapter is not 'my perspective on Reggio's experience and approach', but about my response and others' responses to the encounter with Reggio.

This is an anecdotal, not an analytic, account. My aim is to illustrate the complexities and endeavours of a learning journey in which the map is drawn as new pathways and opportunities are encountered. In learning our business of supporting the learning of young children, children who are inherently capable, eager and researchful, we are still endeavouring to work out 'what to do'. We're still working out what the 'good questions' are. We are in the process of remembering, re-evaluating and questioning. What does it mean to be a reflective pedagogue? How do we take responsibility to fashion our professional environment in the best interest (however we see that) of children's growth and learning?

How do we learn to value, articulate and profess our professional insights, at a time when the demands of many different agendas are tussling with 'early childhood services' in the UK? How do we enable children to be visible in all of this?

When I began to address the challenges which writing a chapter such as this presents, I was confronted by the questions not only of *what* to write, but also of *how* to write. This is an account of journeys, personal and professional, and although out of sequence, I begin by remembering a reflection made recently – a reflection on the challenge and reward of risk, in the personal aspect of my professional journey.

Spring 1999

On the plane from Newcastle to Reggio. My third visit, this time as group organizer for 130 practitioners, development officers and lecturers from across the UK: the first study seminar for the UK hosted by Reggio Children. Opening the free paper, I found a picture in an article entitled 'A Wanderer Above the Sea of Fog' by Caspar David Friedrich. I asked myself, Is this who I am too? Who we are? Are we also attempting to grapple with and make sense of a sea of fog?

We all were, and are, travellers – expectantly on a journey to meet with renowned colleagues and their service, to see what we could see, but also seeking to clarify, to challenge, to embolden our own directions, goals and aspirations. We were hoping to hear, see, encounter, touch, to make exchange, to find new ways of seeing and understanding who we, professionally, were and are; we were going to open up again our sometimes dusty boxes of dreams, take them out, examine them afresh and sense their value, much as children do alone and together, in their own learning and growing.

Mary-Jane Drummond, at a conference following the Reggio visit, spoke powerfully of journeys and of maps:

> A good tourist guide is what we need to guide us in our journey of becoming good educators. In negotiating highways and byways she hints at curious encounters and new discoveries and asks 'What use is it to us, to have only a motoring map with a big fat blue line, impelling us to speed up it, never knowing, actually, where we are or where we might go? And what use are we then to the children whom we presume to educate!? Driving headlong down the goals-oriented motorway, we miss the wealth of possibilities to either side.
>
> (Drummond 1999)

In writing this chapter, and at the risk of over identifying with Friedrich's wanderer, I am intending to stay 'personal' – to sense that it is important to acknowledge and value the presence of the personal in the realm of professional development. It is so important, and not easy, to stay attached and engaged in our lives as educators; to stay motivated and informed by the adult professional 'I' that sees, learns, thinks and feels for herself and himself. Especially so, maybe, in a professional climate in which, it seems, educators are not often encouraged to think, and in which motorways are built by accountants.

In learning and reading of the perceptions of Reggio's early childhood educators, I have been struck by their acknowledgement of their need to learn for themselves what their 'job' is, who they 'are', and who their children 'are'. One of their most valuable gems, for me, is an emotional intellect in their work, the combination of intellectual and emotional integrity in their task of creating educative environments. They have learned to be researchers and learners, makers and actors, not stage-hands to a pageant of received wisdom.

Many types of journey recently encountered, and paths trodden, came to mind as I sat on the plane thinking about Friedrich's picture – personal journeys, journeys to meet others, journeys with colleagues.

1995: a personal journey, backpacking

I had, for ten years, worked and learned in a popular local authority nursery school, along with committed colleagues, guides and teachers, enthusiastic, eager children, and a supportive and varied community of parents. Whatever age-group of children I was working with, I was mindful of developing peer-learning opportunities for exploration within the learning society and in the children's encounters with the world. Here is a small extract from my review of my work as a teacher of a pre-3s class:

> A key aim must be to develop in the children their individual confidence and skill in the social context of the group in which they've found themselves: on entering the class, the children have a new, exciting and rich resource – each other – and through the developing of their relational skills, the children will also be motivated to acquire the cognitive skills that the resources of the classroom promote. They'll acquire these within the context of fun, eagerness, communication, and with a sense of being in charge, choosing, experimenting.

Jigsaw

Towards the end of a sunny morning, Danielle had sat down at the large table to try out a new, complex 12-part jigsaw I'd put there. She had removed the pieces and was puzzling over them, testing them in different places. Michelle, Emma and Sarah were playing at the nearby home corner.

After a while, Michelle, who was also quite confident with such jigsaws, came over. She sat on the table, leaning towards Danielle, and the two were quickly engaged in 'what goes where'. She was almost immediately followed by Emma and Sarah, who also sprawled out over the table. They swiftly became an animated group keen on the task in hand, swapping and sharing ideas.

As my colleague Anna and I watched them, it occurred to us that in another frame of mind we might have disrupted this group quite early on – 'get off the table!'. Are imperatives of child development, and 'common-sense necessities' of control, in conflict with one another (Duckett 1997)?

Many exciting developments occurred during the 1990s – fruitful early explorations of Highscope principles and methods of 'plan, do, review'; developing our teamwork approach and skills; the redevelopment of our wooded play area; the development of a parent-run family centre in the nursery grounds; the pre-3s classroom. The 1990s were exciting, challenging, and of course sometimes difficult times. For me, it was my 'vocational university'. Brain and human development research was increasingly validating the importance of supported early learning experiences (Trevarthen 1995). Yet much of the 1990s were characterized by a new politicization of education, the effects of cuts, and equivocal valuing by political administrations of what preschool education had to offer. It was a time of 'mums' army' , of cuts, of assimilation of 4-year-olds into Reception, and of political questioning of the value of play as a crucial and pivotal learning methodology. The voices of educators, of researchers, in defence and advancement of 'our children' and 'our service', appeared to go unheeded. While professional understandings and aspirations were growing, this was not matched by a social valuing of young children or early childhood services – quite, it seemed, the reverse.

The Saltwell Towers Project

In the face of my discontent, I perceived an opportunity to describe and develop an integrated early childhood centre which could demonstrate something of the potential of creative early childhood practice, in a good enough, reflective environment. There was, in a local Victorian park, the ruins of a large, castellated house which had lain for 20 years a ruin. It seemed an ideal opportunity for regeneration, an ideal and magical environment, and in a district where early childhood provision was in demand. With the generous financial support of a private trust, I took a year's sabbatical, and, with a small supportive steering group, made a full description of my plans as an application to the new Millennium Commission. Here is an extract from an article written at the time:

> We were keen to be active participants in helping shape the future of early years' services: we wanted to fan the winds of change, not be blown about like ships in a storm! The research was centred on a real location with achievable possibilities. This was chosen for its outstanding environmental quality, its broad, mixed community, and for its possibilities to attract mixed capital and revenue funding. To test the concept, architects, landscape designers, and early years consultants worked together to produce a fully costed description for an ambitious, integrated centre.
>
> The keys that seemed to unlock the possibilities were: a high quality of location and architectural approach; development in partnership; integration of 'care, education and recreation'; a commitment to early learning process and practice, and ongoing professional development; a broad community base – and creative thinking.
>
> Duckett (1996: 22)

Key elements in tackling the issues of environmental and pedagogical design included:

- Acknowledging and supporting the explorative and creative aspects of the early childhood experience.
- An overarching perspective acknowledging children as competent, dynamic, capable and social learners.
- Maximizing the environment as an enabler of creativity.
- Describing researchful, reflective professional practice which would better enable staff to support children's thinking and learning.
- Encouraging social coherence, communication and exchange as a central curriculum characteristic.
- A reflective, built curriculum co-constructed between children and adults, with the necessary concomitants of 'open-ended' time.
- Involvement of carers/family in developing learning environments and situations, as well as care (making practice of the principle that 'parents are their children's first and continuing educators').

In seeking to illustrate our vision, we were keen to refer to practice elsewhere which shared elements of these principles. Tina Bruce's 'principles of early childhood education' (1987: 9) gave us strength, as did information from The Centre for Experiential Education, Belgium (Laevers 1995). The Pen Green Centre was a strong reference, as was The Ark Cultural Centre in Dublin. The strongest and most astounding reference, however, was discovered in accounts of the Reggio preschools. I had heard something about them previously and, at the beginning of the design process, a group of overseas students who had recently visited Reggio gave us an extremely enthusiastic account of their experience. As I read more (e.g. Edwards *et al.* 1993), my astonishment, curiosity and excitement grew. Here seemed to be an entire embodiment of our idea. We weren't inventing the wheel or swimming against the tide – here was an experience that had been persistently and courageously growing during the past 30 years!

Unhappily, the local council eventually decided to opt for a more general option for the building use. However, we had achieved a central goal, which was to demonstrate that this quality of service was actually achievable.

1997: meeting up with others along the way – hosting 'The Hundred Languages of Children' exhibition in Newcastle

During the development of the Saltwell Towers Project proposal I was able to visit places, to read, to listen to lecturers and researchers and to be advised by them. This was an opportunity that, as a working teacher, had been hard to come by. It was in itself a powerful experience – encountering others and being able to reflect on ideas, experiences, attitudes and theories. It emphasized to me the importance of dialogue and encounter in developing and promoting valid, respectful early childhood practice.

An irresistible question emerged: Why not show Reggio's exhibition in Newcastle? Surely this might help others understand, more broadly, what it was we were trying to achieve through the Saltwell Towers Project, and in general? It was hard to convince my colleague, then Newcastle's Early Years Development Officer, to sign up to the idea. She and I had worked together in school some years before and I knew we shared views on the fundamental principles of early years education. 'This is lovely,' she said, 'but you'll never get the money to do it. In early years we can't talk this language any more, it's too out of tune with the ethos of the times – it's something we used to be able to do, but we've lost it.' But once we both committed ourselves to the task of making the idea a reality, we found that we hadn't 'lost it'. In fact, as we drew supporters, funders and colleagues into the project, we found that the spirit that it promoted was akin to that of very many people and many organizations.

Visitors to the exhibition, having negotiated the cultural and language differences, discovered many treasures. Here is a sample of visitors' comments:

A four-year-old in my group only began speaking a couple of weeks ago: in the shadow section she talked non-stop, naming all the objects, and even put on a little show herself.

> (Visiting group leader)

A wonderful experience and inspiration which will hopefully influence my work with children.

> (Primary teacher, Cumbria)

A million more connections for the 'only connect' way of learning. Thanks for the inspiration.

> (Newcastle community arts worker)

Thank you for giving me the chance to see such an inspiring exhibition, which will certainly colour my work in the future.

> (Teacher, North Shields)

Our carnival events, project work in local preschools, and work with children at the exhibition were great fun. Many colleagues are actively engaged in new thoughts and exchanges, new experiences and research as a result of the experience.

There are many consequences locally, from the work of showing the exhibit. My own work project has changed and grown; it has become focused on supporting networking and change both locally and nationally, and on developing new opportunities for developing creative learning environments.

From a beginning where it felt I had rather stepped towards the edge, to 'swim against the tide', I have currently a great sense of being part of a thinking, eager and very rapidly growing band of colleagues. There is a sense of an emboldened 'frontier spirit'.

1998: Journeying with colleagues

- Twenty-two early childhood educators from the region visited the Reggio preschools in 1998, followed later by others.
- A local network of educators and artists for discussion and exchange has become established, working to develop professional capacities in supporting young children's learning experiences. This network has a mixture of functions, including support, exchange, practical development, challenge and sociability. Its current focus is on the development of enabling environments, on developing awareness of documentation in building reflective curriculum practice, and on exploring the various aspects of 'what Reggio is' that are attractive and fundamental in the development of our own practice.

- We are developing new links with the Reggio-inspired projects and networks in Scandinavia, and visits are beginning there, also. We hope that these will become reciprocal.
- Creative projects, characterized by collaboration and reflection, are being developed, often involving educators working together with artists. Many of these are becoming long-term associations, backed by opportunities for reflection and process evaluation. We are learning the habit and benefit of presenting our accounts of children's experiences, of our engagement in their learning processes, and of the ongoing and often surprising projects that are developing.
- The regional arts board is engaged in an ongoing early years priority initiative, aiming to bring artists and educators together in developing understanding of, and creating new opportunities for, creative practice in early childhood education.

Some examples of recent projects or investigations

Young children's creative thinking in action

This is a three-year project supported by the Arts Lottery, currently in its second year. It was developed by the SightLines Initiative in association with Early Education. The project is aimed at creating significant new opportunities for, and experience of, creative approaches to communication, exploration and expression, within a wide variety of early years settings across Northern England. Art forms used are mostly those of visual representation, though a multidisciplinary approach is encouraged. Dance/movement and story-making also feature importantly.

The general aim is to use the combined expertise of artists and educators to engage with children's own explorations of their world in social, cognitive, physical and emotional areas. There is a focus on supporting communication between children. Representation, or 'creation', is approached as a tool for deeper comprehension or exchange of ideas, rather than as an ultimate goal. Our 'desirable outcomes' or 'early learning goals' are new understandings and new relationships reached through close attention to process.

There are two main components in the work with children, both backed by evaluation and reflective processes:

- The ongoing 'school'-centred work.
- A one-month interactive event, 'The Fantastic Attic', for young children at the Discovery Museum, Newcastle, in the middle year of the project.

This project aims also to be a significant training and practice development exercise for practitioners – both educators and artists – in a field which recent conferences and audits have identified as lacking in consistent, informed expertise. There is, comparatively speaking, very limited experience of 'artistic input' with very young children as a tool for developing the children's own creativity and expression. Where such 'arts input' has occurred in the past, it has tended to be led by external, adult-led themes and assumptions. Throughout the project, there is an emphasis that the project will be itself a learning experience, and not deliver a pre-packaged programme. Developing 'best practice' will need to be incorporated into the context of learning how to 'see' and 'listen' to the languages of children's explorations. Practitioner training which accompanies the project is linking theory and practice, and is rooted in the experiences of the project as it unfolds.

Here is an extract from a presentation by the head of a day nursery at the end of the first year:

Staff are taking a new role, not having to direct play all the time, but standing back, seeing how play develops and then intervening – this is a skill that has to be learned the same as all skills. Quite often when nursery nurses qualify and come into a nursery, they see their role as directing play, and it takes a certain amount of self-conviction and understanding to be able to step back and think 'this is where I intervene, this is where I can be useful in my job, but I don't have to dominate it'.

The sort of artwork and creative work in the nursery at that time [before the project] was very adult dominated, even to the point where we had had a nursery nurse get a hand, dip it into paint, press it on as if to say, 'this is a hand print, this is valuable art' – it wasn't. It said nothing of the child . . . we have moved on quite a lot from that and I have seen some really significant changes from our initial start . . . In fact it is exciting and the last session I was involved in . . . I actually saw 'free flow play' in action and it is exhilarating – it actually makes your flesh creep with the excitement of seeing children engaged so much in learning, in fun, in laughter, in social interaction, and role-play.

Creative work . . . is to do with space, it is to do with concepts, it is to do with building, to do with maths, to do with science, things working together – all that is happening, but the most amazing thing for me is that these children are just having a brilliant time.

If you think back to what you really enjoyed in your childhood, it was really good play – it wasn't being made to do sums was it? It was when you had had a really good play session when your mam had let you turn the table upside down and you made it into a ship, and you sailed off to an imaginative land. You don't forget those things. Those are the things that make you a creative person, give you inside your head ways of interpreting stories, ways of thinking about life and ways of interacting with other people. It starts with little ones and how they explore their world.

(Shannon 1999)

The Rising Sun Woodland Preschool Project

This project has been an ideal opportunity in which to develop the challenges and opportunities of an emergent curriculum which supports and builds children's theorizing, communication, imagination and exchange. A local nursery class inhabit a quiet, wooded area of a local countryside centre for one day a week, supported by a team including the centre's education officer, an artist-enabler, and myself, along with the nursery staff. Here is an extract from our initial outline of the project:

> For many decades, the natural environment has been an exciting daily classroom for many Danish children. They have the opportunity to live, learn, grow and explore in specially situated and resourced 'forest kindergartens'. These kindergartens are a resource for urban and rural children alike: they give children a sound basis for respect, understanding and guardianship of the natural world, as well as a rich resource for social and cognitive growth.
>
> In developing its educational culture, the teachers will also draw upon the internationally recognised approach of the Italian preschools of Reggio Emilia, where the teachers' focus is to develop the children's powers of hypothesis, communication, exploration, perception, imagination, invention and creativity.
>
> This will be an unequalled opportunity to live and learn, to be in the natural environment, not simply to visit it as a stranger.

This project is financially supported by a Health Action Zone. As a team, we aim to observe and support the many project threads and enthusiasms that come from the children's exchanges and observations, in their engagement with the environment. It is hard to delimit the realms of engagement – scientific, imaginative, social, ontological – and of course they are often a mixture. Sometimes our interventions encourage close observation, sometimes skills-building. Sometimes, and often most rewardingly, they are provocations in the realms which we adults would regard as imagination or fantasy. Some projects become of interest to the whole group, some remain the interest of just a few, or an individual.

The children have not only encountered many seasonal changes, but have thought about them and interpreted them in many different ways: here are some early experiences:

Talia: Come here with me. I'm brave, come on I can go in here. It stinks when it's deep. Squashy mud! [*In song*] It's splashy when it's deep, splashy on your feet.

[*Walking down to the quarry with a group of children.*]
Luke: Quick, pull in your ears. I can hear something . . . it's a robin.

[*Going down into the quarry. It starts to drizzle.*]
Andrew: Its raining. The sky always gets dark then it rains. It always rains when it's dark, that's why it rains a lot at night.

[*The pond is iced over.*]
Carl: Ice is for melting it melts with the sun. It's made out of sand.
Kath: What does it turn into?
Carl: Nothing. It just goes into nothing. Write that down, that's really important.
Nicola: It's glass and it's squidgy when you stand on it.
Kath: Why?
Nicola: Because it's turning into water.

[*The ice on the pond is all broken up, Theo is pushing his stick around in the icy water.*]
Theo: Ice is munchy. There's a snow monster in there – an ice monster.
Kath: What's happened to the ice?
Theo: Ice monster melted it with his machine. He keeps it in the cave over there [*pointing to the bushes*]. The ice monster makes the ice. [*Pushes his stick under the broken ice again and again*]. I'm going to find the ice monster!

The following comments were made by Heather, the mother of Frazer, one of the children involved in the project:

A few weeks before the start of the project when the crocuses were out, he was picking the crocuses to give to the rabbit and I had to stop him, you know.

But [now] he was screaming at Buzz, the rabbit, for eating his precious daffodils, he was absolutely horrified, pushing the rabbit and putting him back in his hutch, told him he was a naughty boy, put his cover over him, he was really like, very cross and then he was just sitting there crying, picking this dead bit of flower up, he'd only eaten the flower and half of the stalk . . . so I told him it was still green and it would still grow back, but he was very cross with the rabbit . . . that was quite strange, especially when he'd been picking the crocuses and snowdrops a few weeks before to feed to the rabbit.

My sister's got a big pond and she brought a little jar of tadpoles for him, and Frazer just screamed at her . . . We didn't know what

was the matter, at first we thought he was frightened of them . . . But
he really screamed 'cos they had nowhere to live. He thought we
were being nasty to the tadpoles. 'You're being cruel,' he was saying.
'Would you like to live in a jar?' And baby tadpoles don't live in
jars, we had no water to put them in and how they would die
because they need homes . . . so . . . we built a pond at the weekend
and he helped dig out all the soil . . . we've bought loads of plants at
the garden centre for them to hide in and he made little holes for
them to hide in case they were frightened, if the cats came near.

1997 onwards: journeys with colleagues across the country

The interest among the UK early childhood community in 'encountering
Reggio' mushroomed, of course. Many voices, fresh and experienced,
shared the enthusiasm of the advocates of the London and Newcastle
exhibitions. For example, Moss (1998: 3) wrote: 'Reggio can be seen as
a prism or lens, through which we can look at pedagogical work in
Britain and fashion our understanding of early childhood in new ways'.

The strong groundswell of interest continued throughout the UK. The
fellowship of interest was evident in the popularity of the UK study
visits to the Reggio preschools, and the ensuing networking and professional development activity across the UK (Calder *et al.* 1998). In the
guide to the 2000 exhbition Fawcett (2000: 1) writes:

> What you will experience in this exhibition . . . will also remind you
> of the intensity, the joy, the probing curiosity, the creativity of
> children everywhere, as they learn about the world. It is not helpful
> to think of the Reggio preschools as a new educational recipe . . .
> every preschool, through their own observations [should] develop
> their own unique culture and research approach. What we can and
> should do is to examine Reggio's powerful ideas, and consider their
> potential in the UK for redeveloping early childhood services with
> fresh insight.

For me, there is a new sense of the importance of finding out 'what
the good questions are'; of discovering what it is to have an image of the
'competent child', rather than an image of the 'needy child'. There is a
new spirit of exchange and networking, of people being invited to share
new experiences at conferences, and to share their experiences and
thoughts at professional development events. There is a sense of being
adventuresome, just as children are. This is not a new concept. Perhaps the
newness, to me, is simply the sense of dynamic optimism and openness
in the interweaving activities occurring in early childhood environments

across the country, and of being effective in this. If we have an idea it is up to us to share it, examine its potential, give it away, make it happen. To make real the possibilities of 'the resourceful child' here in the UK, we need to continue to build a 'resourceful profession'. Maluguzzi (1995: 28), founder educator of the Reggio preschools, stated that:

> Our goal [in Reggio] is to build an amiable school (and also a hard-working, inventive, liveable, documentable, and communicable school; a place of research, learning, reflection and revisiting), where children, teachers, and families feel at home . . . It must embody ways of getting along together, of intensifying relationships among the three central protagonists.

Perhaps our goal too, could be to build an amiable profession, and also a hard-working, inventive, liveable, documentable and communicable profession; a profession of research, learning, reflection and revisiting.

References

Bruce, T. (1987) *Time to Play in Early Childhood Education*. London: Hodder & Stoughton.

Calder, P., David, T., Drummond, M.J. *et al.* (1998) *Exploring the possibilities of Reggio Emilia: Outline of A Proposal for a British Project*. London: Early Education.

Drummond, M.J. (1999) The Steiner Schools. Paper presented at 'Visions and Choices in Partnership' conference, University of London, 12 October.

Duckett, R. (1996) *The Saltwell Towers Project*. Newcastle: Newcastle Community Insight.

Duckett, R. (1997) From strength to strength, in P. Gura (ed.) (1997) *Reflections on Early Education and Care*. London: Early Education.

Edwards, C., Gandini, L. and Forman, G. (eds) (1993) *The Hundred Languages of Children – The Reggio Emilia Approach to Early Childhood Education*. Norwood, NJ: Ablex.

Fawcett, M. (2000) *Brief Exhibition Guide: The Hundred Languages of Children UK 2000 Tour*. London: Sightlines Initiative/Early Education.

Laevers, F. (1995) *Basic Book for an Experiential Pre-primary Education*. Leuren: Centre for Experimental Education.

Malaguzzi, L. (1995) History, ideas and basic philosophy, in C. Edwards, L. Gandini and G. Forman (eds) *The Hundred Languages of Children – The Reggio Emilia Approach to Early Childhood Education*. Norwood, NJ: Ablex.

Moss, P. (1998) *Exploring the Possibilities of Reggio Emilia*. London: Early Education.

Shannon, R. (1999) Young children's creative thinking in action, Unpublished transcript of presentation day for first year's projects. Newcastle: Sightlines Initiative.

Trevarthen, C. (1995) *Towards an Education Based on Relationships*. London: Early Education.

12 A journey into reality

Kath Hirst

It is almost impossible to visit Reggio Emilia without taking away some of the passion embedded in the town and the preschools. This chapter outlines my experiences during my visit to Reggio. It includes observations and discussions of how I came to arrive at my own construction of Reggio, from lectures, tours, visits to the preschools and conversations with the Reggio educators. It will hopefully reflect some of the excitement and passion I experienced and some of the questions raised.

Reggio Emilia, a provincial town in the Emilia region of Northern Italy, has a rural culture with traditional families. The rural area now houses industry also, and the town enjoys a good economic situation. The town is not a tourist centre – 'just a town' according to our guide. However, to a visitor engaging in the Reggio experience, it is not 'just a town'. The people are full of passion and a determination to create 'a new atmosphere'. We were there on Sunday, 25 April, which was the anniversary of the end of the Second World War in Italy. Outside the grand historic theatre, there was a large gathering of people including many older men. We later learned that this meeting was to commemorate and celebrate the ending of the war, and many of the older men were war veterans. The war was still raging in Kosovo and it was clearly in people's minds.

Large banners, making declarations for peace, had been made by the children in Reggio preschools. These hung from the pillars of the theatre. Later in the week, in the preschools, we saw evidence, in the form of children's drawings and writing, that discussions had taken place between the adults and the children about war and the importance of peace.

A 'tour of the town'

Our tour on foot, on the Sunday afternoon, highlighted the patriotism, culture and passion in the town that makes Reggio what it is. Our guide, whose children had attended one of the preschools, was one of the 'Friends of Reggio'. Our tour started at the theatre, outside which the meeting had been held in the morning. Inside the ancient theatre, it was proudly pointed out to us that the gold leaf and frescos were the originals. Five levels of gold-painted ornate boxes enhanced the horseshoe shape of the theatre, which housed mainly opera, ballet and orchestral concerts. The theatre was also used as a workshop where costumes could be made and scenery painted. The stage was larger than the auditorium. We heard how Pavarotti would be performing there in the year 2000, to celebrate his debut in the theatre 40 years ago. This culture was part of the essence of Reggio preschools.

There was a culture of 'community' too – all the *piazzas* in the town, and there were many, were meeting places for the people of Reggio, especially on a Sunday afternoon. Families and friends met, chatted and went on their way. After the hub of the late afternoon chatter, the *piazzas* would become silent and almost deserted, until they came to life again as a market-place of a Monday morning.

This 'tour of the town' has been included here to provide a flavour of this historic place and of the passion of its people. It is against this backdrop that the children of Reggio are educated, and this inheritance is significant in the particular preschools of Reggio.

The philosophy behind the Reggio preschools

The philosophy and work of Loris Malaguzzi, a highly esteemed educator and philosopher, had a great influence on the philosophy of the Reggio infant–toddler centres and preschools. He epitomized his view of children and childhood in his famous poem. The following is an extract:

> The school and the culture
> separate the head from the body.
> They tell the child:
> to think without hands
> to do without head
> to listen and not to speak
> to understand without joy
> to love and to marvel
> only at Easter and Christmas.

(Filippini and Vecchi 1996: 3)

Malaguzzi's passion is still alive in the Reggio educational experience in the municipal infant–toddler centres and preschools, and his words above sparked many questions such as, 'How often do we as educators inadvertently "steal ninety-nine" of the child's "hundred languages?"' and 'Are we part of the "school and culture" that "separates the head from the body?"' Reggio educators do not refer to subjects or areas of learning but they are all there to be seen when visiting the preschools and observing the adults and children who spend their time there. The question in my mind as I observed the children and adults in Reggio was, 'Should adults impinge on a young child's experiences by bringing such a subject-based curriculum into their consciousness, or should they allow the child to have holistic and deeply meaningful experiences without the imposition of an adult structure?' As we impose our 'curriculum' on young children, do we 'tell them to think without hands, to do without head, to listen and not to speak, to understand without joy, to love and to marvel only at Easter and Christmas'?

The Reggio experience

Progressive thinking and a commitment to research and experimentation are strong characteristics of the municipal Reggio Emilia early childhood system. There is a keen emphasis on staff development and training. The organization of the work is based on collegiality, the presence of the *atelierista* (artist) and the essential participation of families and community members. The environment is an important aspect of this experience. All the centres are very light, with many mirrors, artistic artefacts and plants. On entering the preschools there is a feeling of freedom, an image of the child who is the 'subject of rights', and evidence of an educational experience that aims to develop all their languages, 'expressive, communicative, symbolic, ethical, metaphorical, logical, imaginative and relational' Filippini and Vecchi (1996: 13). The Reggio experience promotes the right of the child to choose, make connections and communicate. It allows freedom for children to think, experience, explore, question and search for answers. It presents a creative celebration of children's work. It is believed that the school has a responsibility to offer the right to creativity, the right to doubt, the right to make mistakes, the right to confront problems and the right to solve problems. The Reggio school is not a school *for* childhood, it is a school *of* childhood. One of the key concerns of the Reggio philosophy is that, from birth, a child should be fully engaged in being part of the world. Carlina Rinaldi, the pedagogical director of the Reggio infant–toddler centres and preschools, emphasized that if you move from the child as a subject of *needs*, to a subject of *rights*, you change completely.

The educators believe that learning is two-way; there is a quest for knowledge not only from the child but from the educators too. They were eager to learn from the child and from us, the visitors, also. The enthusiasm and commitment of the staff was apparent in all the centres. There was obviously a stringent selection procedure in place for all the adults employed in the centres, be they cooks or *atelierista*.

All aspects of a Reggio preschool revolve around the *piazza* that is found by the entrance. This is an area that is used as a 'meeting place' for small or larger groups of children. Materials and clothes for use in dramatic play are here as well as a triad of mirrors. Children can crawl into the mirrored tetrahedron to be alone, or with a few other children. Here they can see different images of themselves and hold their own private conversations. Most classrooms are reached from the *piazza*. There is a common large space and smaller, more discrete areas in each. These smaller areas are provided to give children the opportunity to be alone if they so wish. Children naturally congregate in small groups and are allowed to choose their own space. That Reggio philosophy is about relationships, curiosity and communication was apparent.

Children are not taught formally to read, but many were reading and writing before they went to school at 6 years. This, we were told, stemmed from a child's desire to read and write and a wish to communicate. Posting boxes and a choice of writing materials provide the opportunity for children to send and receive messages. Children use their name, a photograph or other materials of their choice as their 'signature'.

In one preschool, two children's ideas of a map had been developed by the teacher, and children were creating their 'town' from paper, boxes, wood and other materials available. The teacher was watching, listening and, when appropriate, engaging in discussion with them. In the Anna Frank School we observed 16 3- or 4-year-olds sitting in a circle with the teacher, each with their own maps. The teacher called this their 'assembly time' – it was like a meeting! This 'meeting' was seen as a time of evaluation and self-evaluation of their own and other children's work. Children could share their work and be frank about their own and other children's work. The teacher explained later how one child had said to another, 'I don't think your map is very good', but had followed this up with how the map could be improved. This kind of sharing and support was encouraged and not seen as negative criticism but as an important aspect of 'evaluation'. The teacher used a tape recorder so that she could later reflect on the session and decide on future work.

The teacher later told us she was not sure where the project was going. The direction depended on what would emerge when she and colleagues evaluated the morning's discussion. Not all children have had the same experiences. It is not the intention of Reggio that all children have the same experiences at the same time. The philosophy shared by teachers is that those children who have not had a particular experience have not 'missed out'. They will encounter it elsewhere in another experience.

Projects in the Reggio experience are constantly revisited. An illustration of children's earlier work on a map project is to be found in Filippini and Vecchi (1996: 22). The children had the following to say about their map of Reggio Emilia:

The city was built by the stonemason.

Its name is Reggio Emilia.

The city never dies because it's made of air, sun, bushes and clouds; and it doesn't have any blood. It only breaks down when there's a war.

These quotes illustrate the children's awareness of their surroundings and the openness and frankness of the adults as they develop children's awareness of the horror of war. Projects in the Reggio preschools can last over a two-year period and are revisited with different children.

Our question might be, 'What were the children learning?' This is a question the Reggio educators also ask themselves, but, I feel, with very different interpretations which allow for, as Malaguzzi wrote:

a hundred thoughts
a hundred ways of thinking
of playing, of speaking . . .

. . . a hundred worlds
to discover
a hundred worlds
to invent
a hundred worlds
to dream.

(Filippini and Vecchi 1996: 3)

My construction of Reggio

I took away from Reggio a deep respect for the Reggio educators. They never cease to search for an understanding of the child's world. Malaguzzi pointed out that the art of research dwells in the hands of the children, and they are keenly sensitive to the pleasure of wonder. Helping children in the Reggio way provided opportunities that enabled them to understand their experiences which 'lead them to knowledge and how knowledge produces more knowledge' (Filippini and Vecchi 1996: 36).

Malaguzzi also reminded us that we, as adults, need the same freedom that we are seeking for children, with as much competence, imagination and curiosity as children demonstrate. The educators in the Reggio experience did not claim that they had all the answers. On the contrary, they were all constantly asking questions and seeking to communicate even more closely with the child and its 'hundred languages'.

Carlina Rinaldi clearly stated in one of her lectures, 'Your Reggio is not my Reggio' (Rinaldi 1999); the values cannot be copied, lifted to another situation, another culture. The powerful images, concepts and qualities that are the bedrock of the Reggio experience are retained in each person's 'Reggio'. As one educator said, 'It's a big commitment'. The child (and the adult) need to feel whole. The 'hundred languages' enable them to feel so.

Malaguzzi stated that 'today's children' expect a pleasure of understanding, learning and knowing from any experience, even when reality may prove that 'learning, knowing and understanding involve difficulty and effort' (Filippini and Vecchi 1996: 34). The child's capacity for survival enables that transformation of 'pleasure to pure joy'. My 'journey into reality' reawakened my senses to all I believe of childhood, and made me affirm that I would try not to look for solutions before I have asked the questions, thereby robbing children of 'ninety-nine languages'. Indeed, if we listen to children, they confirm there are a hundred!

References

Filippini, T. and Vecchi, V. (eds) (1996) *The Hundred Languages of Children: The Exhibit*. Reggio Emilia: Reggio Children.

Rinaldi, C. (1999) Our experience is only one possibility. Paper presented at Reggio Children conference of British delegates, Reggio Emilia, 22–6 April.

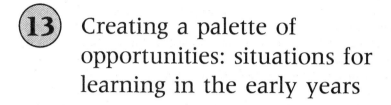

Creating a palette of opportunities: situations for learning in the early years

Cathy Nutbrown

Childhoods and adulthoods: beginning questions

This chapter explores what children in the early twenty-first century might need from their early planned preschool experiences in order to lead full and satisfying lives as world citizens. It is necessarily conceived from my own values, and my own assumptions about what is 'good': that peaceful coexistence is better than war, but that it is also important to be prepared sometimes to 'fight' for one's values and principles; that having enough is better than living in poverty; that health is better than illness; that balance is better than excess, of one thing or another. Balance – between the arts and the sciences, between wanting and having, between giving and receiving, between certainty and uncertainty, between joy and despair – is an essential curriculum ingredient. Balance, and love; love being a necessary condition for living – for health, for well-being, for learning, for achievement, for relationships and for community.

So what do young children of the early twenty-first century need from their early educational experiences? What sorts of things might be good for them to do? What kinds of adults might be best fitted to work with them? What might their daily planned experiences be like? What kinds of environments would be best suited to their needs and the ways in which they spend their time? These are important questions whatever our working context, culture or country.

To ponder, to any purpose, these questions there are further questions to ask, questions which often remain unasked. These unasked questions centre around adults and their adulthoods. Such questions are ignored because children are often thought of as separate and distinct from adults. Childhood is often constructed as a distinct and distant phase of life from adulthood and the intermediate stage of adolescent life can often be conceived as a necessarily tedious rite of passage from the one to the other (Hazareesingh *et al.* 1989; Goldson 1997). There is no sense of wholeness about childhood and adolescence; rather a sense that these two earlier phases of life are necessary stages towards the goal of *becoming* an adult. Because childhood is often constructed in this way, discussion of children and childhoods rarely begins with discussion of childhoods – unless of course there is something 'wrong' with the adult, in which case childhood can be seen as the source of the 'problem' (Coppock 1997).

The idea of children as 'unfinished' or 'incomplete' has already been expressed elsewhere, and as this chapter will later discuss, directly informs the forms and processes of many early years curricula:

> This concept of the child as an 'unfinished' adult shifts the focus away from the child's own intentions, attachments and strivings – which might in fact open up many learning horizons for the adult, on to an end-product notion of adulthoods which is unwisely equated with 'achieved knowledge'. It might be said that this represents a specifically western, 'rationalist' approach to both childhood and learning which by separating the mind from the heart, effectively denies the essential unity of the child.
>
> (Hazareesingh *et al.* 1989: 18)

This chapter begins with the premise that questions about the nature of provision for children need first to confront underpinning questions of citizenship. That is to say, we need to ask, what kinds of adulthood do we seek to create for the early twenty-first century? What do young adults of the early twenty-first century *need* in order to lead full and satisfying lives, to be citizens who contribute to and receive from their world? What sorts of thing might such people *do* in their adulthoods? Who will they spend their time with? What will their daily lives be like? From the world which they inherit, what kind of world will they create and inhabit?

In its report on citizenship the Department for Education and Employment (DfEE) (1999) quoted extensively from the submission from the British Youth Council (BYC) which represents almost 100 youth oganizations and some 3 million young people aged between 18–25 years. The BYC commented:

> The curriculum should address issues such as democracy, community, society and citizenship.
>
> It should look at what representative democracy is, how it evolved, what it means and what its advantages and disadvantages are. It should also look at other political systems around the world and other

representative democracies. The curriculum should also emphasise the importance of citizenship at a global level and show how people can be exploited when they don't understand citizenship.

It should consider the responsibility of belonging to society – the rights and responsibilities of citizens. It should look at children and young people's rights and responsibilities as citizens, and how these change as they grow older. It should also look at the law and the justice system and how it relates to their rights and responsibilities.

The curriculum should enable children and young people to develop an awareness of community and cultural diversity. It should help them see where and how they fit into the community. It should enable them to understand their community, its history, what part it has played in national life etc. It should also enable them to gain an understanding of the diversity of community and society and an awareness of equal opportunities issues, national identity and cultural differences. In addition, the curriculum should show how ordinary citizens have been catalysts for change and improvement at a local, national and international level.

The curriculum should consider the factors that lead to exclusion from society, such as bullying, colour and other forms of difference. It should make students aware of the difficulties such exclusion can have on the individual and society and of the reasons why some people opt out of the moral social set-up.

In looking at these areas, the curriculum should enable children and young people to explore and understand key questions, moral problems and issues that concern society.

The curriculum should also cover practical skills that enable young people to participate effectively in public life and prepare them to be full citizens. It should enable children and young people to develop discussion, communication and teamwork skills. It should help them learn to argue cogently and effectively, negotiate successfully and co-operate with others. It should also enable them to think for themselves, solve problems and make decisions effectively.

(DfEE 1999: 4–5)

Many early childhood educators will identify in the above statement some key elements of an appropriate early years curriculum, such as:

- The responsibility of belonging to society.
- The rights and responsibilities of citizens.
- Developing understanding of their community and how they fit into the community.
- Developing an awareness of: community and cultural diversity; equal opportunities issues; factors that lead to exclusion from society (such as bullying, colour and other forms of 'difference').

- Developing: an ability to explore and understand key questions, moral problems and issues that concern society; skills of discussion, communication and teamwork; the ability to argue cogently and effectively, negotiate successfully and cooperate with others; the ability to think for themselves, solve problems and make decisions effectively.
- Developing practical skills that enable young people to participate.

All of the above points – paraphrased from the words of the BYC can be translated into realizable opportunities and interactions as part of a curriculum for children in the early years.

So, having stated at the outset that 'balance' is a key constituent of curriculum, what kinds of early experience would provide opportunities for young children to grow into world citizens who would, as Robert Fulghum (1986) wrote, 'live a balanced life'? What kinds of early experience with what kinds of adults, in what kinds of environments would enable young children to grow into adults who live and work in enriching company? What kind of community of learning and learners might young children need to help them make the most of their childhoods – to learn about being citizens of their communities, countries and their world – while they reach towards the individual and collective tomorrows of their adulthoods?

These are searching questions which few in the UK of the early twenty-first century pause to ask. In the rush to understand, interpret and enact the latest policy change, many early childhood educators have been allowing (or battling against) the erosion of the space they need to ask questions which penetrate the depth of their work. Questions such as, 'What are we aiming for?', 'Why are we doing this?' and 'What kind of future do we want for our young children?'

So, given my conviction that adults of the twenty-first century will live better lives as world citizens if they understand the need for peace (and seek negotiation and coexistence as a pathway to a state of peace); given my premise that *balance* and love, in living and learning are present in all our strivings and desires; given these things, what kinds of early preschool group experience might be offered to young children? Given that children's childhoods are not solely 'preparing states' of time in their lives, but can, for each child, be a present and powerful state of being *in themselves*, with their own mix of drudgery and struggle and ease, branding experiences of love and pain, delight and fear; given that childhood as childhood can be valued *as* and *of* and *for* itself, what do we do with the question 'What is early childhood education for?' We could answer this question by saying that it is for *now* and for *later*. But, crucially, what happens now so impacts upon what happens later, that the two questions about 'What kind of children do we want?' and 'What kinds of adult do we want them to be?' are inescapably entwined. Perhaps we could go so far as to say that they both ask the same thing?

So, here I shall explore some of my fundamental questions of purpose, in much the same way as an artist might build up a series of sketches, and mix swatches of colour as they work towards creating a painting.

A palette of opportunities

So what kind of palette of opportunities might we create for young children in preschool education? What do they *need* when they learn? Here the discussion draws on examples from UK and from Reggio Emilia preschools and infant–toddler centres in Northern Italy, to explore what might be offered to children in terms of two kinds of opportunities. The first might be described as those deeply embedded elements of heritage: history, community, culture, values and vision. These could be considered as the primary colours on a child's palette of early education. The secondary hues might include those more locally defined elements of space, materials, time, and people. These primary colours and secondary hues of opportunity mix and blend in different ways, and in composition they serve to create experiences for children in early childhood education.

The metaphor used for this in the New Zealand early education curriculum was that of a mat (*Te Whariki*) where all have certain essential elements, but others were added to each individual 'mat' of learning depending on interests, needs, culture, community and so on (New Zealand Ministry of Education 1993). I want to suggest that the composition of the palette of a child's early educational opportunities will depend upon what exists from heritage in the primary colours, and those secondary hues derived from different visions of what childhood is about, what it is, what it is for, what kinds of adult the world needs and what kind of world its citizens create.

The primary colours: heritage, history, community, culture, values and vision

I stood in the central *piazza* of Reggio Emilia on 25 April 1999. The speeches in front of the 100-year-old Municipal Theatre marked the anniversary of liberation from occupation at the end of the Second World War. Animated conversation between groups of older men, and the prominence of families with young children walking and talking together signalled a key event in the history and heritage of the country. It struck me then that the nurseries of Reggio Emilia were born out of the experience of oppression, and the connection with the Women's Movement. Their desire to make something better for their children led to the birth of a movement which eventually gave rise to the 13 infant–toddler centres and 21 preschools of Reggio Emilia. Witnessing the events in the *piazza* that sunny Sunday morning signalled the beginning of my learning that Reggio *was* Reggio because of its heritage, and because of the desire of the women that its community turn oppression into a new experience for children. History pointed to the need for something different in children's earliest years so that they would grow into adults who held community and citizenship as central to their being. There is, I think, an inescapable emotion connected to the development of Reggio Emilia provision for young children, and my experience of those centres was that emotion is a necessary prerequisite for understanding. Attempts to divorce feeling from the intellectual engagement with Reggio ideas would probably be impossible and, ultimately, unproductive.

The Italian tricolour was 'born' in the town hall of Reggio Emilia on 7 January 1797, with white for peace, red for love and passion and green for hope and the future. The document celebrating 200 years of the Italian tricolour states: 'That flag and that symbol were to follow the fortunes of both the City and of the country. Over the centuries the inhabitants of region have had recourse to these same principles of liberty, fraternity and equality which inspired those who first raised this flag' (Artioli 1998: 1). Aware of this symbolism, we can understand something of the national heritage and aspirations for the future which underpin the work upon which Reggio Emilia preschools were built.

Rich multicultural heritages in the UK can also be drawn upon to create preschool experiences with deep and well-established roots. Heritages of landscape and architecture, art and music, dance, folklore, religion, science and invention, stories and poetry, climate and changes. Heritages from local communities which explain traditions, reactions and suspicions.

Recent UK educational heritage includes the Plowden Report (CACE 1968) with its famous declaration: 'at the heart of the educational process lies the child'. In 1989 the Rumbold Report (DES 1990) legitimized the use of the term 'educator' and recognized the multiple types of provision for young children. It is when heritages such as these are forgotten and the past denied, and fresh starts attempted with no acceptance of history, that early childhood education flounders. It cannot be cut off at its roots, and can only be successfully be regrown from existing stock in well-prepared and nourished soil, or as Abbott and Moylett express it, early education can be 'transformed' not 'reformed' (1999: 4).

The secondary hues: space, materials, time, and people

In the 1990s, much was written about creating environments for learning for young children. There are many descriptors of desirable space, materials, time and educators (Jackson and Goldschmeid 1994; Whalley 1994;

Abbott and Moylett 1997; Anning 1997; Duffy 1998; Hurst and Joseph 1998; Nutbrown 1999; QCA 1999). There is broad agreement that children need appropriately designed and dedicated space in which to play and explore. They also need a variety of materials to enable them, as they interact with others, to explore, create, discover, ask questions and solve problems. Giving children time is perhaps more contestable, and there is a sense from current national initiatives that in the drive to raise standards of achievement there is a rush to perhaps over-accelerate learning through the early years of childhood (Nutbrown 1996, 1998). Much work has also been carried out on the importance of appropriately qualified people (Abbott and Moylett 1997; Abbott and Pugh 1998) and the need for very young children to have a 'key' worker' in their daycare setting (Goldschmeid 1994).

Of course, establishing agreement on the importance of children's space, materials and experiences, time and people is one matter – reaching agreement or understanding about the blend and mix of these hues of experience for individual children and families is another. We need to recognize that the mixing of each individual child's palette of early education will be different. They may begin with the same pigments to draw on but different amounts in different combinations will produce different results. So in providing children with space, materials, experiences, time and people we offer opportunities, and each child's use of these opportunites will depend on how children are able to access what is provided. We can provide children with the 'paint', but only they can paint their 'picture'. Alongside the issue of 'access' to the curriculum is the difficult task of mixing the priorities set by government with our belief in what young children need. There are times when the two are compatible, but there are other examples when the promotion of formal teaching of literacy and numeracy to 4-year-olds threatens to stunt the creativity and enthusiasm for learning in other facets of their lives and interests.

The question is perhaps, 'What drives our curriculum?' And again we return to the questions at the beginning of this chapter. We can ask again, 'What kinds of adults and adulthoods will the present system create?' Or better, 'What kinds of adults does the world need, and how do we best nurture them as children?' These are fundamental questions for early childhood educators. They supersede any discussion of space, time or qualifications, because they are questions which reach into the heart of the purpose of education, and the construction of communities which will carry young children into their adulthoods. The aim must be, in the words of the BYC, to 'teach them responsibility, help them to understand diversity, argue cogently, negotiate successfully, think for themselves, make decisions effectively' (DfEE 1999: 4). Courageous and clearly articulated decisions must underpin the creation of situations for learning in early education.

Blending the palettes of Reggio and the UK

This book is essentially about what can be learned from the Reggio Emilia experience which will usefully contribute to the development of early childhood education in the UK. Dialogue between educators across national boundaries offers opportunities for fruitful exchanges. As those who open their doors to international visitors in Reggio Emilia express it:

> Meeting and sharing with others means re-thinking ourselves and re-discovering the sense of what we do; moreover, comparing thoughts and ideas on the theme of education means recognising that the issue of young children can bring the world together, and being active in the education of young children can contribute to the creation of a new culture of childhood that goes beyond any national or cultural frontiers.
>
> This is especially true for us here in Reggio Emilia. During these seminars and institutes, our city, by virtue of its experience, becomes a central meeting place for different cultures and a stimulus for exchange. But the experience also provokes new questions, new ideas, and new possibilities for Reggio, precisely because we are part of the dialogue. Asking ourselves new questions means acknowledging that our experience is constantly evolving – a journey in progress – and it is wonderful for us to know that we have so many travelling companions.
>
> (*Rechild* 1997: 9)

It must be acknowledged that, just as different systems apply in Reggio and the rest of Italy, different systems and experiences exist in the UK. This has always been the case and, with the establishment of the Scottish Parliament and the Welsh Assembly during 1999, the differences in early education provision influenced by need, vision and culture will become more obvious. One example of the difference in emphasis between state perceptions of appropriate curriculum between England (and Wales) and Scotland was to be found in the consultation documents on curriculum for children aged 3 to 5. For England and Wales the emphasis was on goals, outcomes and 'future learning' with little reference to play and enjoyment.

> The high priority given to the expansion of good quality early years education places reflects the Government's determination to raise standards in schools, in particular in literacy and numeracy, and its recognition of the importance of early years education in laying secure foundations for children's later learning.
>
> (QCA/DfEE 1999: 2, para. 2)

In contrast, the Scottish consultation document *A Curriculum Framework for Under Fives* offeres a different emphasis:

> The starting point for all learning is the child and this requires a recognition of the particular experiences which children bring to the early years setting and the ways in which these are fostered and developed. For adults this involves negotiating the balance between the younger child's struggle to achieve independence and their need for ongoing emotional support.
>   Play is, of course, a crucial part of learning at this stage.
>
> (The Scottish Office 1998: 4)

But how might the palettes of Reggio Emilia and the various regions of the UK be blended so that the finer colours and hues of both experiences are drawn out for all children to use and enjoy in a blend of early education experiences? Central to the expression of philosophy at the Diana School at Reggio Emilia are issues and practices based upon 'rights':

The rights of children
The fact that the rights of children are recognised as the rights of all children is the sign of a more accomplished humanity.

The rights of teachers
For the teachers, each and every one of them, it is a condition that enhances communication and the comparison of ideas and experiences, all of which enrich the tools of professional evaluation.

The rights of parents
Participation and research are, in fact, two terms that summarise much of the overall conception of our educational theory. These two terms might also be seen as the best prerequisites for initiating and maintaining a cooperative understanding between parents and teachers, with all the value that is added to the educational prospects of the children.

(Malaguzzi 1993: 2)

Issues of rights have been tentatively explored in terms of early education in England (Nutbrown 1996), but their discussion is not central and it is unlikely that they will feature in many school prospectuses.

Mirrors and masks: moments of learning

Visiting any early childhood setting is a privilege, as indeed it was to visit the Reggio Emilia infant–toddler centres and preschools. *Pedagogistas, atelieristas*, parents and children allowed us to witness their work and discuss with them the intricacies of their thinking which led to the kinds

'The mirror faces'

of practice which were compellingly meaningful. Observations of course are so personal, and interpretation of what is seen depends upon the eyes through which those observations are made. This section is therefore a reflection of my own experience of those encounters during a single week of visits, lectures and discussions – my own construction of Reggio 'as I saw it'.

Mirrors

There are mirrors everywhere in the Reggio centres. They fill large corners of rooms, they hang from the ceiling and they dangle in small fragments from mobiles made by groups of children from recycled materials. They encourage looking – looking at oneself; they make reflections, and in some cases multi-reflections of the same image through mirror after mirror after mirror. The presence of so many mirrors invites personal reflection on oneself, one's work and one's own observations and assumptions.

Through the mirrors of Reggio Emilia centres I saw much that I recognized and much that makes sense in terms of what I believe is 'right' for children. I saw many of my own values, and many of my principles in practice. I also saw much of the excellence of teaching young children that can also be seen in many nurseries and early childhood centres in the UK.

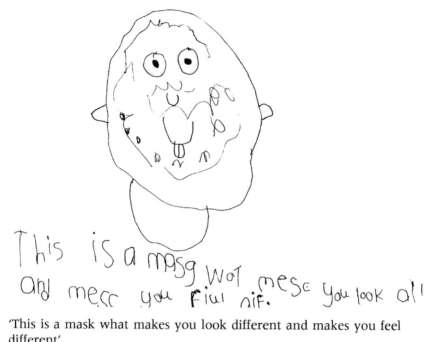

'This is a mask what makes you look different and makes you feel different'

Masks

A workshop on the theatrical mask run by two Reggio Emilia practitioners described how children from one of the preschools were taken to a production of *Giselle* in the theatre and how they later explored the attributes and uses of a theatrical mask during sessions in the preschool. The workshop was compelling, with vivid descriptions of children's experiences with the masks which change, cover and disguise and which make the wearer 'feel' different. The metaphor of the mask also carries a message for early childhood education in countries where there is a state of change and difficulty, where some values are not shared or understood, and where there are different ideas of what counts as important for children and their childhoods. The metaphor of the mask bears a message, a warning that those who work with and for young children should be careful about those threats which disguise what is good about what they do. Early childhood educators need to take care not to unwittingly adopt masks of imposed language, imposed principles and imposed pedagogy which profoundly alter their feelings and well as their practice. Moreover, they also need to take care not to wear mask after mask, changing their own identities as educators as pedagogic fashion dictates.

Our understanding is rooted in our own worlds, including our inter-pretations and lived experience of citizenship, creativity and heritage. The language we use to discuss our understandings is often colloquial, engaging only others who speak as we do; however, we also need to learn to speak an international language of early education in order that early childhood education might increasingly be part of an ongoing international conversation.

Niente senza gio'ia

As early childhood educators internationally seek to create rich palettes of opportunities for young children, we would do well to remember the words posted in the entrance to the Diana School at Reggio Emilia – there were written the words of children who had been discussing the NATO bombing of Kosovo:

War . . . is a rule that shouldn't exist.

(Alessandra 4.11 yrs)

The daddies, mommies, and children get their feelings hurt by war.
(Giorgia 4.2 yrs)

War isn't good for anything, it's not good for thinking.
(Giorgio 6.1 yrs)

It's a real war, not just on television. Whoever started the war doesn't know when to stop it.

(Sara 4.4 yrs)

Amidst the children's words about the war in Kosovo there was another poster which stood as a testimony to the early years of childhood and which we could do well to adopt as a central tenet of pedagogy in the early years. It read, *'Niente senza gio'ia'*: Nothing without joy.

As early childhood educators in the UK work towards inclusive and international understandings of early childhood education, may they do so in a spirit where they incorporate pleasure and satisfaction in their pedagogy:

'Niente senza gio'ia' – 'Nothing without joy'.

References

Abbott, L. and Moylett, H. (eds) (1997) *Working With the Under-3s: Training and Professional Development.* Buckingham: Open University Press.

Abbott, L. and Moylett, H. (eds) (1999) *Early Education Transformed.* Buckingham: Open University Press.

Abbott, L. and Pugh, G. (eds) (1998) *Training to Work in the Early Years: Developing the Climbing Frame.* Buckingham: Open University Press.

Anning, A. (1997) *The First Years at School* (2nd edn). Buckingham: Open University Press.

Artioli, L. (1998) *1797–1997: The Two-Hundredth Anniversary of the Italian Tricolour.* Reggio Emilia: Local Authority of Reggio Emilia.

CACE (Central Advisory Council for Education (England)) (1967) *Children and their Primary Schools* (Plowden Report). London: HMSO.

Coppock, V. (1997) 'Mad', 'bad' or misunderstood? in P. Scraton (ed.) *'Childhood' in 'Crisis'?* London: University College London.

DfEE (Department for Education and Employment) (1999) *Citizenship.* London: DfEE.

Duffy, B. (1998) *Supporting Creativity and Imagination in the Early Years.* Buckingham: Open University Press.

Fulghum, R. (1986) *All I Really Need to Know I Learned in Kindergarten.* New York: Villard Books.

Goldson, B. (1997) 'Childhood': an introduction to historical and theoretical analyses, in P. Scraton (ed.) *'Childhood' in 'Crisis'?* London: University College London.

DES (Department for Education and Science) (1990) *Report of the Committee of Inquiry into the Quality of the Education Experience Offered to 3 and 4 year olds* (Rumbold Report). London: HMSO.

Hazareesingh, S., Simms, K. and Anderson, P. (1989) *Educating the Whole Child – A Holistic Approach to Education in Early Years.* London: Building Blocks/Save the Children.

Hurst, V. and Joseph, J. (1998) *Supporting Early Learning: The Way Forward.* Buckingham: Open University Press.

Jackson, S. and Goldschmeid, E. (1994) *People Under Three: Young Children in Day Care.* London: Routledge.

Malaguzzi, L. (1993) *'Identity Card' of Diana.* Reggio Emilia: Reggio Children.

New Zealand Ministry of Education (1993) *Te Whariki: Developmentally Appropriate Programmes in Early Childhood Services.* Wellington: Learning Media.

Nutbrown, C. (1996) *Respectful Educators, Capable Learners: Children's Rights and Early Education.* London: Paul Chapman Publishing.

Nutbrown, C. (1999) *Threads of Thinking: Young Children Learning and the Role of Early Education,* 2nd edn. London: Paul Chapman Publishing.

QCA/DfEE (Qualifications and Curriculum Authority/Department for Education and Employment) (1999) *Early Learning Goals.* London: QCA/DfEE.

Rechild (Reggio Children Newsletter) (1997) Professional development without frontiers. Reggio Emilia: Reggio Children.

The Scottish Office (1998) *A Curriculum Framework for Under Fives.* Edinburgh: The Scottish Office.

Whalley, M. (1994) *Learning to be Strong.* London: Hodder & Stoughton.

14 The otherness of Reggio

Peter Moss

Introduction

This chapter mainly consists of a paper I gave at a seminar held in Reggio Emilia in June 1999. The theme was learning and teaching and children's learning processes, and as I said at the time, I felt very much a 'learner' myself. Although I had once visited Reggio in the 1980s, on that occasion I understood very little about the pedagogical work there. Some understanding, and I emphasize the 'some', has only come in the last two or three years, through having the opportunity to work with a Swedish colleague, Professor Gunilla Dahlberg, who has had a long and deep relationship with Reggio, as well as to take part in a study visit with a group from Britain.

For the reasons set out below, I see Reggio as an important, but not a generalizable, experience. We cannot escape responsibility for making our own choices about early childhood by 'buying in' to a 'Reggio pro-gramme': for the choices we face are political and ethical, not between competing programmes or 'models of good practice'. At a time in Britain when a rhetoric of choice and diversity in the provision of early childhood services is matched by the application of a range of 'human technologies' (Rose 1999) intended to secure increasing standardization in practice and purpose and to normalize our thinking and doing, one reason why Reggio is so important is that it reminds us that it is possible to think and do differently – that there are many different ways of working with young children, and indeed evaluating that work.

It is not that those in Reggio are right, and we in Britain are necessarily wrong. Rather, Reggio self consciously *chooses* to work within a particular paradigm, aware that such a choice has certain consequences. In Britain on the other hand there is a lack of paradigmatic self-awareness, and instead a search for absolutes: the right way, best practice, quality, excellence. While we seek *the* answer which will enable us to foreclose, in Reggio they understand that even after 30 years or more, their work remains provisional, continually open to new conditions, perspectives, understandings and possibilities.

Were the early childhood services of Reggio to wake up one morning and find themselves transported to Britain, they could expect no great welcome or support from the government. From an official British position, Reggio does not fit and therefore can be easily written off, without any attempt at understanding. Reggio breaks all the managerialist rules that shape Britain's approach to the development of early childhood services. It has managed to develop a world-renowned pedagogical project, drawing thousands of visitors and inspiring services in countries around the world, without the benefit of prescriptive guidelines on content or methods, quality assurance or accreditation schemes, inspection systems, Baseline Assessments or other 'outcome' indicators or research. Even worse, the services are provided by the local authority!

Unlike those nice (usually American) studies which reduce things to numbers, and purport to 'tell' us how things really are and therefore what we have to do, Reggio asks us to engage in a process of co-constructing understanding, to make our own interpretations and judgements as to the value of its work. While Reggio asks, and expects us to ask, many critical questions, the government in Britain asks only one question – 'What works?' – and recognizes only one approach to evaluation, situated within what has been termed the 'modernist project' with its epistemology of logical positivism, its belief in stable criteria, its assumption of the objective social scientist and its distaste for philosophy and moral issues. Reggio's approach is perhaps nearer to that discussed by Bill Readings (1996), when he speaks of evaluation as an act of judgement and self-questioning, embedded within a context that must be acknowledged. He argues that evaluation produces a judgement of value, which should not be confused with a statement of fact; furthermore, the judge must take responsibility for that judgement rather than hide behind claims of statistical objectivity. Readings is at great pains to emphasize the provisionality of evaluation as judgment: in other words, the importance of keeping the issues open and subject to continuing discussion rather than seeking to close and finalize the matter. According to Readings, 'the question of evaluation is finally both unanswerable and essential'.

None of this is intended to give the impression that Reggio is either abstract or woolly. On the contrary, the early childhood system clearly functions very well, offering an excellent service to the citizens of Reggio. The pedagogical work is extremely rigorous and subject to constant critical scrutiny and reflection. The whole emphasis is on contextualized practice – what is going on in early childhood institutions in their particular context – rather than applying abstract and decontextualized guidelines or forms of assessment. Taking the distinction as defined by Cherryholmes (1988: 178–9) one could say that in Reggio they have adopted a 'critical pragmatism', while much of British policy equates more to a 'vulgar pragmatism':

> Vulgar pragmatism holds that a conception is to be tested by its practical effects . . . what is true and valued is what works in terms of what exists. This is another face of instrumentalism in pursuit of production and efficiency . . . This form of pragmatism is unreflective and dangerous . . . Vulgar pragmatism tests ideas and practices by comparing them to traditional and conventional norms with little or no sense of crisis or criticism. Vulgar pragmatists, to draw upon [Umberto] Eco one more time, promote local ideologies as global and past ideologies as those of the present and future . . . Critical pragmatism continually involves making epistemological, ethical and aesthetic choices and translating them into discourses–practices. Criticisms and judgements about good and bad, beautiful and ugly and truth and falsity are made in the context of our communities and our attempts to build them anew. They are not decided by reference to universal norms that produce 'definitive' and 'objective' decisions.

One understanding of Reggio's pedagogical philosophy and practice

What follows is an attempt to understand more of the Reggio approach, originally presented in a seminar on teaching and learning and addressed to the educators of Reggio themselves. The topic of the seminar to which I was invited to contribute was learning and teaching, and children's learning processes. As a relative newcomer to the pedagogical philosophy and practice of Reggio, I felt myself still to be a novice learner, rather than a wise teacher. I therefore decided to go back to an old interest of mine – the 'problem with quality' – and consider how the pedagogical philosophy and practice in Reggio (as far as I understood them) might relate to this subject. I concluded by asking, as a relative newcomer, 'How might we learn in relation to Reggio?'

Let me begin by sketching my understanding of the pedagogical philosophy and practice in Reggio, starting with the concept of knowledge. Knowledge is not the discovery of some inherent truth about the world. It is not finding and representing an objective reality waiting 'out there' to be discovered. Knowledge is not something absolute, existing outside context and unchangeable – and, as such, transmittable to the child. From Reggio's perspective, knowledge is the product of a process of construction, involving interpretation and meaning-making. In the words of Carlina Rinaldi (the recently retired head of early childhood services in Reggio), 'what children learn emerges in the process of self and social construction', and learning is 'the subjective process of constructing reality with others'. Knowledge is perspectival and provisional – and since it involves interpretation and meaning-making, and therefore choices – we must take responsibility for our own learning.

But knowledge is not just constructed and learning is not just an individual act. Knowledge is *co*-constructed, in relationship with others, both children and adults, and in this process listening is critical – listening both to others and to ourselves. 'To listen' is understood to be an active verb, involving not just hearing but interpreting and constructing meaning. To listen in this way means being open to the Other, recognizing the Other as different, trying to listen to the Other from their own position and experience, and not erasing differentness by treating the Other as the same, and by putting our understanding and perspective onto the Other. Hence, Loris Malaguzzi (1993), the first head of early childhood services in Reggio, spoke of Reggio working with a 'pedagogy of relationships', and Carlina Rinaldi speaks of a 'pedagogy of listening'.

There are also many similarities here with the view of pedagogy expressed by Bill Readings when he says: 'I want to insist that pedagogy is a relation, a network of obligation . . . [in which] the condition of pedagogical practice is an infinite attention to the other' (1996: 165). Readings argues for the importance of 'listening to thought' in pedagogical work, for 'doing justice to thought means trying to hear that which cannot be said but which tries to make itself heard'. This, he adds, is 'incompatible with the production of even relatively stable and exchangeable knowledge' (p. 165).

A pedagogy of relationships and listening recognizes and values subjectivity, rather than dismissing it as an obstacle to the higher value of objectivity. It is comfortable with ambivalence, singularity and difference. It knows that knowledge is perspectival, contextual and provisional. Rather than seeking certainty – to fix and foreclose – it strives to hold open meaning: again to quote Bill Readings, a pedagogy of listening 'is to think beside each other and explore an open network of obligation that keeps the question of meaning open as a locus for debate' (p. 165).

Reggio's pedagogy understands knowledge and learning processes in a very particular way. It also understands the child in a very particular way. Reggio starts from a recognition that we construct childhood and how we understand who the child is, can be and should be. Since many possibilities exist, this process of construction involves us making choices and assuming responsibility for those choices. Furthermore, our choices are enormously productive of theory and practice: how society sees children and understands childhood, and its hopes and expectations for children, represent philosophical questions underlying education. It follows that pedagogical work with young children is necessarily a political and moral project.

In Reggio they have chosen to understand the child as rich, competent and intelligent, a co-constructor of knowledge, a researcher actively seeking to make meaning of the world. In doing so, they have decided not to choose other understandings or constructions of the child, which have been very productive in other types of pedagogy and other areas of work with children. For example, the child as knowledge reproducer, the child as an innocent, or the child as nature, 'an essential being of universal properties and inherent capabilities whose development is innate, biologically determined and follows general laws' (Dahlberg *et al.* 1999: 46). Reggio has also rejected the construction of the 'child at risk' or 'in need', not only because it produces a 'poor child' but because they have chosen, in Carlina Rinaldi's words, 'to move from the child as a subject of needs to a subject of rights'.

Finally, the pedagogical practice in Reggio has important tools – for example, pedagogical documentation (for a discussion of this tool, see Dahlberg *et al.* 1999), and the roles of *atelieristas* and *pedagogistas*, as well as an understanding of the pedagogue (or educator) as co-constructor, as researcher, as reflective practitioner. The pedagogue is not a transmitter of knowledge and culture. Rather, he or she is a facilitator in children's co-construction of their own knowledge and culture, through supporting relationships between children, constructing interesting and intelligent situations, asking questions, listening to and respecting children's own theories; but also challenging them, valuing curiosity and wonder. As one *pedagogista* explained to me, the task is to offer a context in which the child can themself explore and go deeper into a problem.

Getting beyond the problem with quality

Let me now change course, to consider quality, although I will return to draw out some relationships between this issue and my understanding of the pedagogical philosophy and practice of Reggio. We live in what might be called the 'age of quality'. Every day the word appears in countless places attached to countless activities, goods and services. Quality is what everyone wants to offer and everyone wants to have. This is very apparent for the field of early childhood services in the Anglo-American world (mainly the USA and Britain), where there is a mountain of work on 'quality'. But I think it is increasingly true elsewhere, including Italy and Scandinavia.

Most discussions about quality concern how it can be defined, measured and assured, assuming that quality is some universal and knowable entity, waiting 'out there' to be discovered and measured, usually by experts. For some years, however, this idea of quality – as a universal and objective norm – has been questioned in the early childhood field because it ignores context and complexity, plurality and subjectivity. Quality, it has been argued, is actually subjective and value-based, relative and dynamic, with the possibility of multiple perspectives about what quality is. Bill Readings' (1996: 24) critique of 'excellence' – a concept much used by Anglo-American universities – could equally well apply to quality and early childhood institutions: 'Measures of excellence raise questions that are philosophical in that they are fundamentally incapable of producing cognitive certainty or definitive answers. Such questions will necessarily give rise to further debate for they are radically at odds with the logic of quantification'.

The 'problem with quality' therefore is this: if quality is not an essentially technical issue of expert knowledge and measurement, but is a philosophical issue of value and dispute, what should we do about it? If quality is not about defining and measuring the one true way, what can be offered in its place? Trying to find an answer to this question has been one theme of a recent book *Beyond Quality in Early Childhood Education and Care: Postmodern Perspectives* that I have written with two colleagues, from Sweden and Canada (Dahlberg *et al.* 1999). There is not the space to present the arguments set out in that book, only to summarize some of our provisional understandings.

In our view the problem with quality cannot be addressed by struggling to reconstruct the concept in ways it was never intended to go. 'Quality', we argue, is not a neutral word, but a socially constructed concept. This concept is produced from a 'discourse of quality', which is itself the product of several related forces, including Enlightenment thinking and a particular rationality found in the world of business. Above all, the concept of quality makes sense within a philosophical framework, a way of understanding the world, what Habermas (1983) refers to as the 'Project of Modernity'. This philosophical perspective has had a powerful hold on the Minority World[1] for more than 300 years. It values certainty, linear progress, order, objectivity and universality. It believes in a knowable world out there waiting to be revealed and capable of accurate representation.

The concept of quality embodies the values and beliefs of modernity and has a very particular meaning – that of a universal, knowable and objective standard. It is an example of what has been called a technology of distance applicable anywhere, irrespective of context, and capable of excluding subjective interpretations. The concept cannot be reconceptualized to accommodate complexity, values, diversity, subjectivity and multiple perspectives.

If, however, you choose to work with complexity, values, diversity, subjectivity and multiple perspectives, *if* you recognize the temporal and spatial context of institutions, *if* you consider pedagogical work to be political and moral – then making sense of or evaluating early childhood institutions requires a different discourse and a different concept, what we refer to as meaning-making. This discourse and concept is self-consciously situated within a different way of understanding the world – the Project of Postmodernity.

From the perspective of postmodernity there is no objective reality waiting 'out there' to be discovered, no external position of certainty, no universal understanding that exists outside history and society that can provide foundations for truth, knowledge and ethics. Instead the world and our knowledge of it are seen as socially constructed and all of us, children and adults, are active participants in the process. The discourse of quality seeks to judge the conformity of practice to predetermined criteria: the discourse of meaning-making, in contrast, is first and foremost about constructing and deepening understanding of the early childhood institution and its projects, especially pedagogical work, to make meaning out of what is going on. From constructing these understandings, people may choose to continue by making assessments about the work – a process involving the application of values to understanding to produce a judgement of value. Finally, people may further choose to seek some agreement with others about these assessments, both about what is going on and its value. However, the discourse does not assume that all three stages must be followed. Indeed, it may be considered sufficient to concentrate on deepening understanding without going on to assess or to seek agreement.

What has this to do with learning and Reggio? I would suggest three connections. First, we can view both discourses – quality and meaning-making – as ways of learning about early childhood institutions. Quality assumes a 'transmission' form of learning: we learn about institutions through the application of predetermined and prescribed criteria. These criteria offer supposedly firm foundations for knowledge of what is good. They are often manifested as scales or other types of measure. Quality, we might say, is related to a pedagogy of conformity and normalization, control and management: terms such as 'quality' 'displace real political and policy choices into a series of management imperatives' (Clarke 1998: 179).

In contrast, meaning-making assumes a process of co-construction of knowledge, an interpretive process in which each person makes their own meanings. It assumes choices must be made and that we must take responsibility for our choices: meaning-making, we might say, is related to a pedagogy of difference and 'dissensus', of dialogic and democratic practice. While quality seeks to foreclose, by reaching a definitive conclusion (often expressed numerically), meaning-making recognizes the negotiated and provisional nature of understanding and assessment because, in Readings' words again, 'the question of evaluation is finally both unanswerable and essential' (1996: 25). Quality therefore represents a theory of learning and knowledge radically at odds with that espoused by Reggio, which shares much in common with the discourse of meaning-making.

Second, the pedagogical practice in Reggio can inform the practice of meaning-making. The process of pedagogical documentation is an important tool; it provides us with evidence and a process for meaning-making. Understanding, as well as assessment, is undertaken in relation to others: it is a reciprocal and dialogic activity, whether understanding the learning of an individual child or the pedagogical and other work of an early childhood institution. There is a role too for what might be termed 'wise helpers' in pedagogical practice and evaluation, whether they be *pedagogistas*, evaluators or some other group.

Third, as I understand it, the work in Reggio has usually avoided the discourse and concept of quality. This makes sense if we recognize that the concept of quality and pedagogical work in Reggio are located within different philosophical frameworks and understandings of the world.

I have hurried through what is a complex debate. In conclusion on this point I would like to add that as authors we are not arguing in *Beyond Quality* that the discourse and concept of quality should be abandoned. Our argument is not prescriptive. Instead, we are trying to apply critical thought to quality, meaning in Foucault's words 'to show that things are not as self-evident as one believed, to see that which is accepted as self-evident will no longer be accepted as such' (Foucault 1988: 155). What we are saying is that 'quality' as a concept is problematic, that it is not neutral and self-evident, and that we all have choices about how we evaluate pedagogical work – and those choices have moral and political dimensions, not least because they are very productive of policy and practice.

How might we learn in relation to Reggio?

I want to conclude by raising a further question about learning: how can those of us who do not live and work in Reggio learn in relation to Reggio? This question is both important and troubling. In Reggio they problematize a common Anglo-American concept – that we can buy and consume a model or programme, and by so doing be reproducers of someone else's knowledge. In Reggio they question the idea of models and programmes, universally applicable because they are context and value free; they say Reggio does not offer a recipe nor a method and cannot be copied because values can only be lived. They tell us that in Reggio they faced many possibilities for early childhood work, each with its own values, and that they made their choice of one to follow, taking responsibility for that act of choice as a consciously ethical and political decision. They point out gently that they have been working on their project for over 30 years and that it is a project without conclusion.

Furthermore, it does not take much acquaintance with Reggio to understand that their experience has been produced from within a very particular political, economic and social context and draws on a very particular historical experience. In his study of Italian regions – which concludes that the Emilia Romagna region is by far the most successful in Italy both economically and politically – the American political scientist Robert Putnam (1993) provides some understanding of the origins of the strong values of democracy and social solidarity that permeate Reggio's work and the importance attached to relationships and dialogue. In particular, he emphasizes the deep reserves of 'social capital' in this part of Italy, produced by, and productive of, trust, mutuality, cooperation and other social values.

Work by Putnam and others also identifies a particular form of capitalist organization that is widespread in this part of Italy, characterized by the clustering of small- and medium-sized companies producing similar products, who manage to combine competition with a capacity to collaborate in matters of mutual interest. This raises another important set of relationships that we easily ignore in discussions of early childhood – but do so at our peril, especially at a time of constant and rapid change. That is, the relationships between childhood and pedagogical work on the one hand, and dominant forms of capitalism in particular places and at particular times on the other.

Once we get over not being able to have a Reggio model, we can open up to other possibilities.

For those of us who live and work in very different contexts, Reggio provides us with a sort of lens for looking at our own situations – in Britain, Sweden, the USA or wherever – a lens which helps to make the invisible visible and to see what is visible in a different light. This can enable us to become more critical thinkers. For example, my understanding of Reggio has helped me to problematize the British concept of the 'child in need', and has increased my awareness of the dominant but 'taken-for-granted' discourse of 'need' in Britain and its consequences for policy and practice (Moss *et al.* 2000). Furthermore, by insisting on the political and moral nature of pedagogy and childhood, involving choices which reflect values, the experience of Reggio problematizes the 'end of history' discourse in the Anglo-American world. This discourse speaks of a world in which there is no longer disagreement about purpose and value, only about the most efficient systems of management for delivering universally agreed objectives. It produces just one question, which currently dominates British public policy: 'What works?'

Working in relation with Reggio opens possibilities for co-constructing new understandings about pedagogical and other work with young children – rather than reproducing dominant understandings. In this context, Reggio educators become co-constructors in processes of producing new knowledge rather than guardians of 'the true faith'. This process of co-construction requires us to make our choices about our philosophical position, to make an analysis of the context within which we find ourselves, and to choose what values are important for us in our work.

We can learn from Reggio the importance of 'border crossing' for early childhood work. For many years, work in Reggio has been informed by a wide range of disciplines and perspectives, enabling its educators to relate early childhood to a broad intellectual culture and tradition. This wide-ranging interest has been productive of a particular philosophical perspective, which informs thinking about children, knowledge and learning. In our book, we suggest that Reggio's 'pedagogical practice is located in . . . a philosophical perspective which in many respects seems to us postmodern' (Dahlberg *et al.* 1999: 122). We realize that those in Reggio would not choose to attach such labels – but perhaps would agree that their work is influenced by a multiplicity and diversity of perspectives and theories.

By contrast, Anglo-American early childhood work remains dominated by one particular discipline: developmental psychology, described by Burman as 'a paradigmatically modern discipline arising at a time of commitment to narratives of truth, objectivity, science and reason' (1994: 18). Speaking from her experience in the USA, Block (1992: 3) observes that:

> the terms critical theory, interpretivist or symbolic research or postmodern are rarely heard in seminar rooms, publications or conferences focusing on early childhood education . . . one reason for [this] lack of alternative perspectives [being] the century-long domination of psychological and child development perspectives in the field of early childhood education.

The issue here is not to reject developmental psychology, but to see it as one type of knowledge out of many that can contribute to our learning processes and hence the construction of new understandings about early childhood.

Finally, I think we can learn from Reggio the importance of small-scale and local experiences. Small-scale and local does *not* mean insignificant. For Reggio shows us how powerful a small-scale but very rich experience can be. It can be a source of inspiration as well as a locus of 'dissensus', challenging by its very existence dominant discourses and practices – and by so doing, keeping the question of meaning open as a locus for debate. So we return here to the concept of a pedagogy of listening, which recognizes and values difference.

If we are to be co-constructors of our own knowledge about young children and early childhood work, not reproducers of others', the importance of creating and maintaining spaces of difference, 'dissensus' and debate cannot be overestimated. In particular, it seems to me that we need to confront the implications of the increasingly hegemonic position of the Anglo-American world, based on linguistic, cultural, economic and technological power. In early childhood, this growing hegemony means the increasing dominance of very particular discourses and constructions about early childhood, early childhood institutions, and learning, which in turn produce very particular policies and practices – all very different from those in Reggio Emilia. Moreover this problem of hegemonic influence is not readily recognized because the Anglo-American world operates within a philosophical position – the Project of Modernity – which believes in the possibility of objective and value-free knowledge producing universal solutions, including global definitions of 'good practice' and 'quality'. In other words, the dominant intellectual paradigm of Anglo-American early childhood work is based on a rationality which renders issues of power, choice and responsibility invisible.

I would add that as part of this process of confrontation we need to deepen our understanding of the form of capitalism that dominates the Anglo-American world and is now becoming increasingly dominant in other parts of the world. I have argued that the pedagogical work in Reggio can be better understood in the context of the particular form of capitalism that has emerged in this part of Italy. But so too can we understand the dominant Anglo-American discourse about early childhood – and the policy, practice and research it produces – in the context of Anglo-American neo-liberal capitalism, which foregrounds the following: free markets and the commodification of all activities and relationships; competition and the necessity of inequalities; contractual relationships with predetermined and measurable outcomes; individual responsibility and autonomy; the primacy of shareholder value and business values; flexible employment and lifelong learning to fulfil the shifting needs of the labour market; short-term time frames and the desire for solutions – to know 'what works'. Correct solutions are valued over critical questions, and, to be correct, solutions must be final, clear-cut and universal: hence our obsession with programmes, best practice, quality and planning.

In these circumstances, it seems to me that those of us from the Anglo-American world who have an interest in Reggio have a particular responsibility to insist upon the 'otherness' of Reggio and the importance of this. We must try to explain this 'otherness', as best we understand it, as well as the opportunities it offers for critical thinking – for giving a new meaning to the rhetoric of choice and diversity so widespread today. We must also try to explain the dangers of importing the demands and expectations of Reggio. This assumes its sameness, and presumes that it shares a neo-liberal rationality. It may also unwittingly undermine its otherness by exposing it to the totalizing influence of Anglo-American power.

This may make it difficult, sometimes impossible, to attract large grants and government interest, at least in some countries like my own. But the prospect of a mass conversion to some Reggio approach or model is neither possible, nor would it be desirable – for that would mean a new dominant discourse, a new priesthood with new technologies of normalization. What may be on offer is a possibility, for those who are interested, of an emancipatory learning – emancipatory not in the sense of freeing people to realize an essential human nature, but emancipatory in the sense of enabling critical thought. The purpose of emancipatory learning can be understood in Foucault's words as 'the art of not being governed so much by power' (1988) and as promoting 'reflective indocility'. This ideal is expressed by a previous mayor of Reggio. Asked why the people of Reggio created an early childhood system around the perspective of the child, he answered that the Fascist experience had taught them that people who conformed and obeyed were dangerous and that in building a new society it was imperative to communicate that lesson and nurture a vision of children who can think and act for themselves. That purpose seems to me to be as challenging, important and relevant today as it was 30 years ago.

Note

1 I use the term Minority World to encompass those countries which are sometimes referred to as 'developed' or 'of the North'; while the term Majority World refers to the remaining countries of the world which account for most of the world's population and area (as defined in Dahlberg *et al.* 1999).

References

Block, M. (1992) Critical perspectives on the historical relationship between child development and early childhood education research, in S.A. Kessler and B. Swadener (eds) *Reconceptualizing the Early Childhood Curriculum: Beginning the Dialogue*. New York: Teachers College Press.

Burman, E. (1994) *Deconstructing Developmental Psychology*. London: Routledge.

Cherryholmes, C.H. (1988) *Power and Criticism: Post-Structural Investigations in Education*. New York: Teachers College Press.

Clarke, J. (1998) Thriving on chaos?, in J. Carter (ed.) *Postmodernity and the Fragmentation of Welfare*. London: Routledge.

Dahlberg, G., Moss, P. and Pence, A. (1999) *Beyond Quality in Early Childhood Education and Care: Postmodern Perspectives*. London: Falmer Press.

Foucault, M. (1988) *Politics, Philosophy, Culture: Interviews and Other Writings, 1977–1984* (ed. L. Kritzman). New York: Routledge.

Habermas, J. (1983) Modernity: an incomplete project, in H. Foster (ed.) *The Anti-aesthetic; Essays on Postmodern Culture*. Port Townsend, WA: Heinemann.

Malaguzzi, L. (1993) For an education based on relationships. *Young Children*, November: 9–13.

Moss, P., Dillon, J. and Statham, J. (2000) The 'child in need' and 'The rich child': discourses, constructions and practice, *Critical Social Policy*, 20(2): 233–54.

Putnam, R. (1993) *Making Democracy Work: Civic Traditions in Modern Italy*. Princeton, NJ: Princeton University Press.

Readings, B. (1996) *The University in the Ruins*. Cambridge, MA: Harvard University Press.

Rose, N. (1999) *Powers of Freedom: Reframing Political Thought*. Cambridge: Cambridge University Press.

15 Questions and challenges – continuing the dialogue

Lesley Abbott and Cathy Nutbrown

We have called this final chapter 'Questions and Challenges' because every question raised in this book creates new challenges, and as we read and reread each chapter, the more apparent this becomes.

Just as those who have visited Reggio Emilia talk about 'my Reggio' so we must leave the reader to take from each contribution what is significant for them in relation to their beliefs about children, about early childhood and the context in which they are working.

What we can do is briefly revisit some of the central concepts which underpin the work of the Reggio educators, and somewhat self-indulgently highlight key examples of the ways in which 'a week in Reggio' has influenced, and in some cases changed, practice.

Here we attempt to revisit what it is that is so distinctive about the Reggio Emilia approach, and take examples or simply key words or phrases from some of the chapters.

We have been delighted by the responses from such a wide range of people to our initial invitation to 'reflect on Reggio'. All of us clearly benefited enormously from the 'total immersion' which we experienced during that week. Some were 'old hands' and had visited Reggio in the past; others felt that through their reading, discussion and the inspiration gained from visiting the 'Hundred Languages of Children' exhibition on its first visit to the UK, they already knew quite a lot; but for some others it was a totally new and challenging experience. During that week, policymakers, practitioners, trainers, researchers, lecturers, managers, architects, artists, politicians and parents visited the Reggio schools, talked with the staff, listened to lectures and discussed with colleagues, bringing their distinctive 'eye' and particular perspective to the process.

Returning to work after some time away, if only on holiday, is not easy to do. We tend to view problems which seem insurmountable, and people who may not be operating on our 'wavelength', with a new eye when sitting on a sun-kissed beach, only to find that things are just the same when we return. What is significant about the contributions you have read is the degree to which changes in perception, policy and practice are already taking place.

In the two years following our week in Reggio we have met with many of the contributors. Some we have known for many years as friends and colleagues, others we met in Reggio for the first time and have since forged strong links and productive working relationships. We can testify to the fact that as a result of this experience children, students, families and communities have benefited. It is however important to remember that for all of us the process of reflection is only just beginning, and as Freire (1996: 108) reminds us: 'new ways of valuing and thinking do not become instituted from one day to the next like magic. It is not like moving a table from one spot in the house to another, in which physical strength is all that is required, changing cultural habits is a different story'. 'New ways of working require a long, sustained and participatory effort' (Penn 1997: 120). We have no doubt that for each of us that effort will continue.

Journeys and maps have been used as analogies when reflecting on Reggio's contribution to our thinking – for example, Drummond (1999), Dahlberg (2000) and Chapters 11 and 12 of this book. It is important that we recognize that our skills and abilities as map-readers will vary and that each one of us is at a different point on the journey. In exploring some of the issues, experiences and practices which have been significant, 'our practice must always be open for rethinking and reformulation and we must learn to live with uncertainty' (Dahlberg 2000: 182).

The central concept in the Reggio approach is the 'rich' child, and throughout this book there are examples of children who are 'autonomously capable of making meaning from experiences' (Malaguzzi 1993: 75). The children in Christine Parker's nursery, who welcome her back and ask 'Why you go Italy Mrs Parker?' (see Chapter 10), and the subsequent activities in which she involves them, help us to recognize with Malaguzzi that: 'Children's self learning and co-learning supported by interactive experiences constructed with the help of adults, determine the selection and organisation of processes and strategies that are part of and coherent with the overall goals of early childhood education' (Malaguzzi 1993: 78).

The Reggio approach is characterized by a variety of pedagogical tools for developing its pedagogical practice in a rigorous, open and dynamic way. The procedure of documentation as a 'democratic possibility to inform the public of the contents of school' (Vecchi 1993: 96) is something which both Parker and Duckett consider important in their work (see Chapters 10 and 11).

In her exploration of the role of the *pedagogista*, Knight, as an early years advisor has discovered, and already put into practice, new ways of supporting practitioners in a variety of settings at a time when the changing context of early years is making increasing demands on them (see Chapter 4).

The emphasis on 'special rights' rather than 'special needs' has clearly challenged Phillips and Nurse (see Chapters 7 and 8) to think about the terminology we use. They raise important questions about what exactly is meant by 'inclusion' and whether in fact this was happening in the schools they visited.

Acknowledgement of the importance of the relationship with parents underpins the Reggio philosophy. It was clear from the schools we visited that strong and effective partnerships have been formed between the institutions and their parents who are actively engaged in management, discussion about pedagogical work and discussions about their children's lives. We have been privileged to have contributions from two parents of 'Reggio children' who have the added advantage of having experienced 'our system' too. The 'extra pocket' and 'invisible gear' which Sunniva and Sam possess as a result of their time in the Reggio schools (see Chapters 5 and 6) is something we would want for all our children. It is when they are no longer needed that we will recognize that Utopia has been reached!

The contributions to this book reflect only a small number of the many issues raised, questions asked and challenges faced by those who visited Reggio Emilia in April 1999. At the end of the week each person was invited to contribute one thought or question to be written on a square which would later form a tapestry of reflections. Some of these are shown in Figure 15.1. Many of these thoughts we will read and merely nod in agreement. Others will provoke us, if not to action then certainly to frame a response. However we respond, it is clear that much has been gained from the opportunity to learn from Reggio.

Educators in Reggio have always sought to locate their pedagogical work in relation to the wider society and to an understanding of the world that children are growing up in. Concern for children's understanding and appreciation of the built environment led John Bishop, as an architect, not to 'make a portrait of a lion' as the children in Reggio had done in the town *piazza*, but to work together with children, teachers and students to engage in and document a project based on Manchester's impressive town hall (see Chapter 9).

This book began with our recognition that Reggio Emilia values its children. Several contributors (Hirst, Scott, Phillips, Nurse) have talked about their feelings on seeing the children's thoughts and words about the war in Kosovo written on banners hanging from the theatre for the whole community to read. Some of these thoughts are shown in Figure 15.2.

Figure 15.1 Questions and challenges for practice in the UK

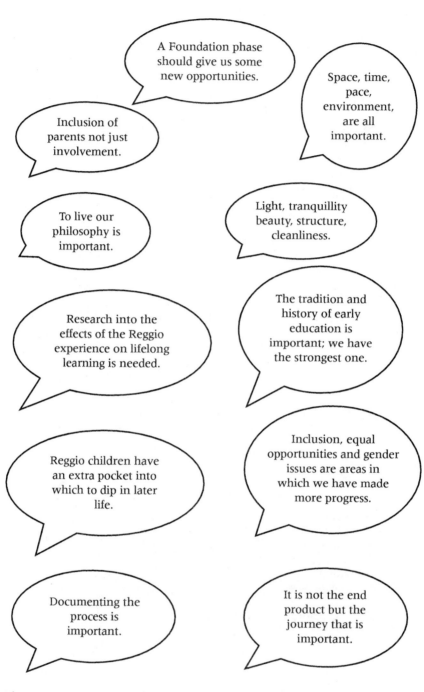

Figure 15.1 *(cont'd)*

Figure 15.2 Children's thoughts on war displayed on banners outside the theatre in Reggio Emilia

Questions offer an opportunity to construct a real encounter.

Transcultural dialogues are important.

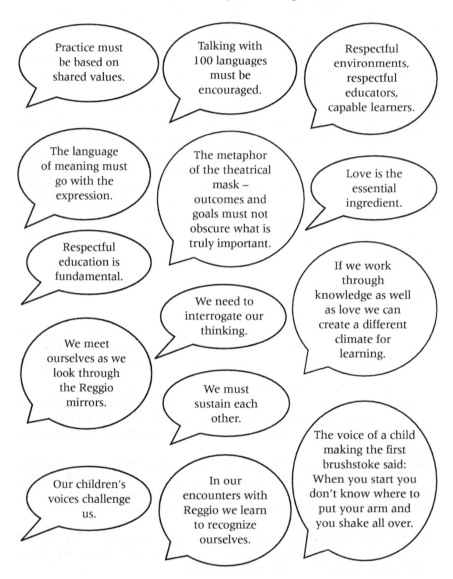

Figure 15.3 Some learning points gained from our encounter with Reggio

Adults' thoughts can be seen in the statements made by the visitors at the end of the visit, shown in Figure 15.3.

In discussing 'the otherness of Reggio', Moss (Chapter 14) reminds us that Reggio does not provide a 'model' or 'programme' and does not want to: their work, as they put it, has been one possibility they chose from many possibilities, and that choice has moral and political dimensions. In considering how Reggio might contribute to our own thinking and understanding, Moss suggests that it provides a lens through which to view and deconstruct our own work, to make the invisible visible, to question the taken for granted and to act as a co-constructor in our process of learning and producing some understandings and new practices.

Throughout the book the name of Loris Malaguzzi, the first head of the early childhood service who died in 1993, is mentioned. It is therefore fitting that we should end by paying tribute to his contribution to early childhood education founded on the perspective of the child: 'Malaguzzi and the other early childhood pioneers in Reggio Emilia have already opened up many new spaces for different conversations about early childhood: we are aware of following behind and of finding those spaces a constant source of inspiration and wonder' (Dahlberg *et al.* 1999: 13).

References

Dahlberg, G. (2000) Everything is a beginning and everything is dangerous: some reflections on the Reggio Emilia experience, in H. Penn (ed.) *Early Childhood Services – Theory, Policy and Practice.* Buckingham: Open University Press.

Dahlberg, G., Moss, P. and Pence, A. (1999) *Beyond Quality in Early Childhood Education and Care: Postmodern Perspectives.* London: Falmer Press.

Drummond, M.J. (1999) The Steiner Schools. Paper presented at 'Visions and Choices in Partnership' Conference, University of London, 12 October.

Freire, P. (1996) *Letters to Christina: Reflections on my Life and Work.* London: Routledge.

Malaguzzi, L. (1993) History, ideas and basic philosophy, in C. Edwards, L. Gandini and G. Forman (eds) (1993) *The Hundred Languages of Children – The Reggio Emilia Approach to Early Childhood Education.* Norwood, NJ: Ablex.

Penn, H. (1997) *Comparing Nurseries – Staff and Children in Italy, Spain and the UK.* London: Paul Chapman Publishing.

Vecchi, V. (1993) Role of the *atelierista,* in C. Edwards, L. Gandini and G. Forman (eds) (1993) *The Hundred Languages of Children – The Reggio Emilia Approach to Early Childhood Education.* Norwood, NJ: Ablex.

# Glossary

Reggio Emilia

asilo–nido: infant–toddler centre. Full-day educational childcare centre for children 4 months – 3 years.

atelier: studio, workshop and art room, furnished with a wide variety of resources and materials, used by all the children and adults in the school. Most classes have their own *atelier* or mini-*atelier* attached to the classroom.

atelierista: teacher trained in art education (artist in residence) in charge of the *atelier*. Works with children, staff and parents, supports curriculum development and helps to produce documentation to contribute to processes of critical reflection on pedagogical work.

educatore: teacher.

pedagogista: pedagogical coordinator. Acts as consultant, resource person and coordinator to several schools and centres. A team of *pedagogisti* serves under the *directtore* (director) who is responsible for the pre-primary and infant–toddler centres.

piazza: communal area and meeting-place at the centre of Italian towns; also the communal area of all infant–toddler centres and preschools.

scuola d'infanzia: pre-primary school. Full-day education childcare centre for children 3–6 years.

scuo'la materna: centre for very young children and infants.

England

advisers: employed by local education authorities (LEAs) to support schools and teachers at a local level.

Baseline Assessment: system introduced in the UK in the late 1990s for assessment of children on entry to school (aged 4), according to nationally prescribed criteria. Due for revision in 2001.

Desirable Learning Outcomes (DLOs): age-related goals for young children to be achieved on entry to school at 5. Replaced in September 2000 by Early Learning Goals (ELGs).

Early Excellence Centres: DfEE designated centres providing integrated services for children 0–5 and their families including training and community support.

Early Learning Goals (ELGs): six areas of learning. 1: personal, social and emotional; communication. 2: language and literacy. 3: mathematical. 4: knowledge and understanding of the world. 5: physical. 6: creative, to be achieved by the end of the Foundation Stage.

Education Action Zone: partnerships between LEAs, schools and business to create greater educational opportunities by developing innovative solutions to local problems.

Foundation Stage: the period from age 3 to the end of the reception year, 5+. A distinct stage and important in its own right in preparing children for later schooling.

Her Majesty's Inspector (of schools) (HMI): inspectors appointed to inspect schools and colleges and report to HM Chief Inspector of Schools.

inspectors: in education, usually refers to Ofsted or LEA personnel appointed to inspect maintained, private or voluntary sector provision.

mentors: those who work in a support and advisory capacity with teachers and other early years staff.

National Literacy Strategy: programme for the teaching of literacy in state primary schools in England and Wales.

National Numeracy Strategy: programme for the teaching of mathematics in state primary schools in England and Wales.

Ofsted: Office for Standards in Education. Government agency responsible for inspection of schools and colleges.

practitioners: generic term often used to refer to adults who work with children in the settings, whatever their qualifications.

setting: the term used to mean childminder networks, LEA nurseries, nursery centres, playgroups, preschools or schools in the state, independent, private or voluntary sectors. Also maintained schools.

Sure Start: government initiative to support families and children before and from birth, particularly those who are disadvantaged.

teaching: refers to all aspects of the role of practitioners. This role includes establishing relationships with children and their parents, planning the learning environment and curriculum, supporting and extending children's play, learning and development, assessing children's achievements and planning their next steps.

Index

EARLY CHILDHOOD SERVICES
THEORY, POLICY AND PRACTICE

Helen Penn (ed.)

This book explores the relationships between theory, policy and practice in early childhood services. Although primarily focused on the UK, it draws on contributions from Europe and further afield to explore the strengths and limitations of present practices and suggest ways in which new initiatives might be developed.

The book considers six interlinked themes:

- How do young children learn? What assumptions are made about children as learners?
- What should young children be learning? What is an appropriate approach to the curriculum for young children?
- Where should young children learn? What arrangements are made for them? What kinds of spaces do children inhabit?
- Who should help them learn? What role do adults take in supporting children's learning?
- Children as participants and knowledgeable persons – what contribution can children themselves make to the plans that are made for them?
- Developing practice – how does practice, particularly embedded practice, change or develop?

The book will be important reading for students undertaking courses in early childhood studies, early years education, social policy and child welfare as well as academics, researchers and policy makers in these fields.

Contents
Introduction – Part one: How do children learn? Early childhood services in a global context – Towards a global paradigm for research into early childhood – Two sides of an eagle's feather: University of Victoria partnerships with Canadian First Nations communities – Part two: What should children learn? Approaches to the curriculum – Te Whāriki: curriculum voices – The future of infant education – Part three: Where should children learn? Space and segregation – The Frankfurt kindergartens – Part four: Who should help children learn? A natural or unnatural profession – The parameters of training – Is working with young children a good job? – Part five: Children as participants – Discipline and normalization in the nursery: the Foucaultian gaze – What is the use of children's play: preparation or social participation? – The rights of young children – Part six: Research and practice – Everything is a beginning and everything is dangerous: some reflections on the Reggio Emilia experience – Research and practice: is there a dialogue? – Index.

Contributors
Pricilla Alderson, Jessica Ball, Roland Burgard, Margaret Carr, Anne Edwards, Gunilla Dahlberg, Chris Holligan, Marta Mata y Garriga, Helen May, Peter Moss, Alan Pence, Helen Penn, Harriet Strandell, Martin Woodhead.

208pp   0 335 20329 9 (Paperback)   0 335 20330 2 (Hardback)

PROMOTING CHILDREN'S LEARNING FROM BIRTH TO FIVE
DEVELOPING THE NEW EARLY YEARS PROFESSIONAL

Angela Anning and Anne Edwards

- What sort of literacy and numeracy curriculum experiences are best suited to the needs of very young children?
- How can early years professionals bridge the current divisions between education and care to provide an approach to young children's learning which draws on the strengths of both traditions?
- How can these professionals be supported as they develop new practices which focus on young children as learners?
- What strategies are most effective in involving parents with their children's development in literacy and mathematical thinking?

Drawing upon research carried out in a range of early years settings, Angela Anning and Anne Edwards seek to address these questions. The emphasis throughout is upon enhancing the quality of children's learning and providing support for the practitioners who work with them. The complexity of addressing the various cognitive, social, physical and emotional learning needs of young children is discussed and practical strategies to develop children's learning are explored with a particular focus on communication and mathematical thinking. Published at a time of dramatic change in pre-school provision in the UK, the book will both inform and reassure early childhood professionals. It will be important reading for managers, administrators and all professionals working in early years and family services and an accessible text for those studying for childcare and education, and teaching qualifications.

Contents

Introduction – Setting the national scene – Integration of early childhood services – The inquiring professional – Young children as learners – Language and literacy learning – How adults support children's literacy learning – Mathematical learning – How adults support children's mathematical thinking – Creating contexts for professional development in educare – Early childhood services in the new millennium – Bibliography – Author index – Subject index.

192pp   0 335 20216 0 (Paperback)   0 335 20217 9 (Hardback)

TRAINING TO WORK IN THE EARLY YEARS
DEVELOPING THE CLIMBING FRAME

Lesley Abbott and Gillian Pugh

In the present context of change and development in the early years field the availability of appropriate training for all those working with young children is of paramount importance. Research shows that one of the most important factors determining the quality of early childhood care and education is the quality of the adults who work with them. The book builds on recommendations made by the Rumbold Committee, the RSA Start Right Report and the National Commission for Education in highlighting key issues, developments and opportunities. More importantly it signals ways in which government policy must change in order to meet the requirements which the authors recommend.

Written by key people in the early years field together with input from students at various stages in their training, the book will be a valuable resource for trainers, students and practitioners concerned to explore ways in which the need for appropriate initial and continuing professional development can be met.

The authors represent a broad spectrum of early childhood establishments, organizations and training institutions both nationally and internationally.

Contents
Early Years training in context – Changing minds: young children and society – Facing some difficulties – Early years educators: skills, knowledge and understanding – Teacher training for the early years – The development of quality services through competence-based qualifications – Praxis NVQ early years assessment centre – a case study: putting the candidate at the heart of the process – Early childhood studies degrees – The pathways to professionalism project – a case study: making an early childhood studies degree accessible – Painting the cabbages red . . . ! Differentially trained adults working together in early years settings to promote children's learning – A European perspective on early years training – Training to work in the early years: the way ahead – Appendix – Bibliography – Index.

208pp   0 335 20030 3 (Paperback)   0 335 20031 1 (Hardback)